FOCUS
ON THE
BANK DIRECTOR

AMERICAN
BANKERS
ASSOCIATION
1120 Connecticut Avenue, N.W.
Washington, D.C. 20036

This publication is designed to provide accurate and authoritative information in regard to the subject matter covered. It is sold with the understanding that the publisher is not engaged in rendering legal, accounting or other professional service. If legal advice or other expert assistance is required, the services of a competent professional person should be sought.

—from a *Declaration of Principles Adopted by the American Bar Association and a Committee of Publishers and Associations.*

Contents

Illustrations

Preface

Perhaps never before has it been so exciting—or risky—to be a director of a bank. Steering banks through the sometimes treacherous waters of deregulation and competition is a challenge and an honor. But, with it, comes the exposure to collective and personal liability that directors take on; exposure that is becoming larger due to the regulators' exuberance and our intensely litigious society.

So it is that the nature of banking and of the environment it operates in causes the bank director's job to be much more than an honorary position. It is a big job getting bigger, and its responsibilities and pitfalls merit updating.

The first edition of *Focus on the Bank Director* was published eight years ago—eight years in a time that has turned out to be the most eventful in banking history. Many of the general philosophies of bank directorship written about in 1977 still apply, but many more of the particulars have changed. New business opportunities, unprecedented competition, financial and economic uncertainty, and industry despecialization and consolidation: these are trends that couldn't help but reforge the board of directors' role. The basic handbook for directors, of course, must follow suit.

The need to revise and update *Focus on the Bank Director* was identified as a priority through the needs assessment process of ABA's Community Bankers Council and Advisory Board. Completion of this book is evidence that the process works and is responsive to bankers' needs.

Thus, we have the all new *Focus on the Bank Director*. Like its predecessor, it is a basic overview of the functions and responsibilities of bank directors. Its primary purpose is to help new directors get started. To that end, it surveys the banking business, explaining the fundamental concepts and terms of bank operations; it describes the general composition and functions of the board of directors; and it highlights the statutory, regulatory, and legal responsibilities assumed by directors, both individually and collectively.

Despite its basic approach and intent, this book is not without use to more experienced bank directors as well. It incorporates the latest information on laws and regulations affecting banks. It is written within the context of today's banking environment, which is so rapidly changing and so radically different than it was only a decade ago that even "old hands" must continually update their understanding.

By the same token, this book is written in general enough terms that directors of small and large banks, national and state banks, will find its contents relevant. Because of its broad applicability, of course, the treatment of some subjects had to be limited. For example, the information on laws and regulations focuses on the federal arena, with the admonition given, when appropriate, that directors should look to their legal counsels to explain specific state laws or advise them on legal questions that invariably arise with respect to the topics discussed.

This, then, is the new edition of *Focus on the Bank Director:* a basic, up-to-date, comprehensive, and widely applicable book on the bank director's job, its characteristics, its rewards, and its problems. Divided into 3 parts and subdivided into 15 chapters, its contents cover the gamut from the mechanics of the commercial banking industry to specific guidelines for helping a director competently manage his or her responsibilities.

During the course of this project, the following senior bank officials and members of ABA's Community Bankers Advisory Board generously lent their expertise, without which, we would not have been able to proceed: G. Rogers Coman, Chairman and President, United Bank of Montrose, Montrose, Colorado; Ronald Duitsman, Chairman and President, University National Bank, Chicago, Illinois; Reed A. Peters, President, The

First State Bank and Trust Company of Larned, Larned, Kansas; and Gene Garrison, Chairman, First National Bank, Alice, Texas.

We also wish to acknowledge Robert Dye, Vice President, Financial Shares Corporation, Chicago, Illinois for his expert guidance throughout this process.

PART I:

The Business of Banking

Part I of this book describes the nature and structure of the banking industry, the products and services that banks provide, bank organization and technology, bank profitability, and bank regulation. The financial services industry is rapidly changing, and this profile of commercial banking must be seen as a picture of something in motion: ongoing developments in competition, technology, regulation, and customer demands will undoubtedly continue and multiply.

Commercial banks are facing dramatic changes in the economic and financial environments. Inflation, the volatility of interest rates, and demographic changes have altered the financial needs of both consumers and businesses. More than ever before, banks are finding that profitability depends on meeting new customer demands for an expanded line of financial products and services. Advances in technology now enable banks to serve their customers more efficiently, yet banks have only been able to expand their services slightly, due to heavy regulation, while non-bank competitors, not bound by similar regulatory constraints, have expanded rapidly. Part I looks at these industry trends and explains proposed regulatory restructuring that will help banks meet their customers' needs effectively and profitably.

1

The Commercial
Banking Industry

The American banking industry is made up of more than 14,000 commercial banks that serve the public as *financial intermediaries*: they provide the means for channeling money from those with excess funds who want to earn interest on their deposits to those in need of funds who want to borrow.

BASIC FUNCTIONS OF BANKING

All banks serve three traditional functions: *accepting deposits, extending credit,* and *making and collecting payments.* In carrying out these basic functions a bank may offer a wide range of financial services. In the typical course of business, a bank may handle deposits, payments, and collections; provide retail, commercial, real estate or agricultural loans; manage trusts; process corporate payrolls; transfer money by electronic wire; arrange for direct deposits of checks to individual accounts; tailor retirement accounts to individual needs; and provide banking services to other banks.

The principal product of banking is money. Banks "sell" this commodity (money) when they lend and invest. To acquire the money necessary for such transactions, banks must secure funds from depositors. Thus, bank customers are both product users and product suppliers. This means that, unlike many other businesses, banks must compete aggressively in the marketplace for the raw material needed to conduct their operations.

The deposit, credit, and payment functions served by commercial banks are vital to our economy. The public uses checks drawn on demand deposit accounts as its principal form of money. In fact, less than one quarter of our basic money supply (funds available for public spending) is cash and currency; the bulk of the money supply is made up of demand deposits. Also, the Board of Governors of the Federal Reserve (Fed) is able to stimulate or slow economic activity by regulating the level of the money supply through the credit and deposit functions of commercial banks.

The Fed requires each bank to keep a percentage of its deposits in reserves to meet its daily operating expenses.[1] After setting aside the required reserves, a bank may lend out the rest of the money it holds. When banks make loans, they increase the level of the money supply (create money) because these loans in turn create new demand deposits. For example, assume that the reserve requirement for all banks is 10 percent of deposits. If $10,000 is deposited in a bank, the bank must set aside $1,000 in reserves and can lend out $9,000. Suppose someone borrows the $9,000 to pay a creditor, who then deposits the money in another bank. After setting aside the required 10 percent in reserves, or $900, that bank has $8,100 to lend out. This process can be repeated, creating new demand deposits (and increasing the money supply) to the maximum amount supportable by cash reserves. In this way, the original $10,000 deposit grows to nearly $100,000 through repeated loans and deposits, creating $90,000 in new funds available for spending. This *multiple expansion of bank deposits* is illustrated in Table 1.

To reduce the money supply, the Fed raises reserve requirements (leaving banks with less money to lend); to increase the money supply, the Fed lowers reserve requirements (providing banks with more money to lend).

Because banking deals in a public commodity, it is one of the most closely regulated, examined, and restricted of all industries. Government regulations cover the type of products and services the industry may provide, the amount that the industry may charge customers to borrow or pay depositors for the use of

Table 1
Multiple Expansion of Bank Deposits in the Banking System
(10% Reserve Requirement)

Position of Bank	New Deposits	New Loans and Investments	Reserves
Bank A	$ 10,000	$ 9,000	$ 1,000
Bank B	9,000	8,100	900
Bank C	8,100	7,290	810
Bank D	7,290	6,651	729
Bank E	6,561	5,904	656
Bank F	5,904	5,314	590
Bank G	5,314	4,783	531
Bank H	4,783	4,305	478
Bank I	4,305	3,874	430
Bank J	3,874	3,487	387
Sum of first ten banks' deposit expansion	65,132	58,617	6,513
Sum of remaining banks' deposit expansion	34,868	31,381	3,487
Total for banking system as a whole	$100,000	$90,000	$10,000
	(Multiple Expansion)	(Net Creation)	(Original Deposit)

Multiple Expansion = 10 Times Reserves

their funds, the operating procedures that the industry must follow, and the geographic areas where the industry may do business.

Commercial banking is an integral part of our nation's free enterprise system. Commercial banks operate over 55,000 offices, employ over 1.5 million people, and hold assets totalling over $1 trillion. All other industries depend on commercial banks for financial services to carry out their daily operations. In fact, virtually all segments of our society (individuals, small businesses, large corporations, not-for-profit organizations, and agencies of local, state, and federal governments) rely on commercial banks to meet their needs for financial services.

Highly skilled and specialized personnel are required to sell and service the scope of financial products available through commercial banks. In addition to specialists in economics, finance, investments, trusts, and international banking, industry personnel include specialists in management, research, public relations, marketing, data processing, and automation.

CUSTOMER BASE

Commercial banks serve retail, commercial, and government customers. Many banks specialize in the type of customers they serve. Retail banks serving the individual consumer usually have many small branches, while wholesale banks serving businesses that require bigger loans and more complex services may have larger branches, but fewer of them.

The industry serves the borrowing needs of its retail customers with consumer loans and residential mortgages, usually competing in this area with thrifts. Commercial businesses borrow to acquire working capital, to meet seasonal or cyclical needs, and to obtain funds for business expansion. Loans to individuals and businesses account for 60 percent of the total assets of all banks. While banks remain the largest suppliers of business credit, corporations now borrow from other corporations through the commercial paper market.

Federal, state, and local government agencies must borrow to meet increased government expenditures. Banks are the largest purchasers of all Treasury bills, notes and bonds, thereby providing indirect loans to the federal government. Bank purchases of municipal debt issues from state and local government agencies provide funds for long-term public improvements that would otherwise require higher and more frequent taxation. Indirect loans to government agencies through securities purchases account for 20 percent of the total assets of all banks.

High inflation and the volatility of interest rates over the last decade, coupled with a greater public awareness and sophistication in personal funds management, have created a new type of bank customer—one not satisfied with idle assets, on the lookout for the highest possible interest earnings, and quick to transfer funds when better opportunities arise. Retail customers now maintain lower balances in their checking accounts, putting their funds to work elsewhere. Similarly, many commercial customers make deposits to cover payments, not when they write checks, but when they expect their checks to be presented for payment to their bank. In order to obtain higher interest earnings, many customers now transfer funds from one account to another within their bank, or to their bank's competitors. Moreover, banks can no longer count on traditional customer loyalty, and must offer quality products and services at competitive rates to hold customer business.

Demographic changes have shaped the new breed of customer as well. The post-World War II baby boom has now come of age, and greater numbers of people are acquiring housing and durable goods. There is also an increasing public concern for securing adequate retirement income, as inflation and declining confidence in the social security system add to the public's uncertainty about the future.

Most importantly, customers today want the convenience of a full range of services from a single supplier, which accounts for the growing number of nonbank firms acquiring banks. The financial service "supermarkets" created by Sears, American Express, the Dreyfuss Corporation, and other nonbank corporations are showing remarkable public appeal. Bank customers are now looking for cash management packages and one-stop convenience. Banks are eager to meet their customers' needs, but can still only slightly expand their services through the use of subsidiaries of the bank or a bank holding company.

INDUSTRY STRUCTURE

The banking industry is not homogeneous; banks differ based on their relationship to regulatory agencies, size, affiliation with parent corporations, geographic distribution, and services to other banks. Banks are formally classified based on their relationship to the regulatory agencies that approve bank charters, and supervise, examine, and restrict bank operations.

The United States has a dual banking system: banks are chartered by either the federal government or state governments. For *state banks*, which make up 70 percent of all commercial banks, charters are approved by state banking agencies; for *national banks*, the chartering agency is the Office of the Comptroller of the Currency. National banks are required to be members of the Federal Reserve System[2] and to insure their deposits with the Federal Deposit Insurance Corporation (FDIC).[3] State banks may be members of the Federal Reserve System, and those not insured with the FDIC account for less than 3 percent of all state banks.

Commercial banks vary in size, from those with assets of less than $1 million to those with assets of over $100 billion. Within the industry there is a high concentration of assets and deposits in a few large banks. In fact, most banks are small businesses: about 90 percent of all banks have assets of less than $100 million. Commercial banks can be classified in four size groups: small *community banks* (less than $150 million in assets); *medium-sized banks* ($150 million to $1 billion in assets); *regional banks* ($1 to $20 billion in assets); and *money center banks* (assets over $20 billion).

A corporation that owns one or more banks is known as a *bank holding company* (BHC). A parent corporation that owns a single bank is a one-bank holding company; a BHC that owns more than one bank is a multibank holding company. Not all BHCs are large multibank holding companies. Most BHCs are created by individual banks that transfer bank stock to parent corporations, allowing the banks to expand their operations by offering added services through the BHC's nonbank subsidiaries. Such expanded services might include mortgage banking, data processing, credit life insurance, leasing, and discount brokerage services.

All BHCs are regulated by the Federal Reserve[4] and, in many states, also by state agencies. The banking subsidiary of a BHC is regulated as an independent bank would be, by the appropriate state or federal agency.[5] Nonbank subsidiaries of BHCs are limited by law to activities closely related to banking.[6] Two-thirds of all commercial banks and bank branches are part of bank holding companies.

Banks may be classified as *unit banks* (single-office banks) or *branch banks*. Approximately 75 percent of the industry's commercial bank offices are branches. The geographic distribution of banks within the industry is governed by state authorities rather than by the federal government. State laws differ, allowing either unit banking, statewide branching, or limited branching. Twenty states allow banks to branch anywhere in the state, twenty-one permit branching within a specified area, and nine do not permit branching at all.

The bank holding company arrangement has provided banks with a means of circumventing state branching restrictions in states that permit multibank holding companies. Through a nonbank subsidiary, a BHC can enter a geographic area that, as a bank, it would ordinarily be prevented from entering.[7] Geographic expansion by banks and BHCs, however, is limited by the Douglas Amendment to the Bank Holding Company Act of 1970. Under this amendment, BHCs are prohibited from acquiring more than 5 percent ownership of a bank in another state unless it is specifically allowed by state law.[8]

The banking industry is able to provide full-service banking in every community because of cooperative relationships between large and small banks. *Correspondent banks* provide small banks with specialized services and information, and enable small banks to take advantage of business opportunities by participating in larger loans than they could make from their own assets. The correspondent bank's services may include providing check processing and data processing services for banks that lack the necessary equipment and facilities, providing international banking services, and providing staff expertise in specialized areas of banking.

MARKET STRUCTURE

The financial services marketplace is highly competitive, and the commercial banking industry faces challenges from a growing variety of competitors. Businesses other than banks that provide financial services can be categorized into two broad groups: *thrift institutions* and *nondepository institutions.*

Thrift Institutions

Like commercial banks, thrifts accept and hold insured demand deposits for the public. Thrifts include savings and loan associations, mutual savings banks, and credit unions.

- *Savings and loan associations* are the largest direct competitors of commercial banks for deposits. S&Ls were originally chartered to provide funds for home financing, and most of their assets are concentrated in real estate mortgages. Most S&Ls are organized as mutuals and owned by their depositors, but some are stock corporations. In 1982, S&Ls held at least 25 percent of the assets of all depository insitutions.

- *Mutual savings banks* are owned by depositors, organized only under state charters, and mostly located in the Northeast. Most mutual savings bank loans are placed in home mortgages. Nationally, mutual savings banks hold about 7 percent of the assets of all depository insitutions.

- *Credit unions* are cooperative associations that deal primarily with member-depositors who have a common bond: for example, employee, military, church, fraternal, and professional groups. The savings of depositors earn dividends and provide funds for member loans. Credit unions outnumber all other depository institutions, but their assets make up about 3 percent of the assets of all depository institutions.

Nondepository Institutions

Nondepository competitors of commercial banks include consumer finance companies, mortgage companies, life insurance companies, money market funds, securities firms, and retailers, among others.

- *Consumer finance companies* compete with commercial banks for retail and commercial installment loans, *mortgage companies* for commercial and residential mortgages, and *life insurance companies* for residential and commercial mortgages and for corporate and individual pensions and annuities. Each type of institution may be acquired by a bank holding company.

- *Money market funds,* first organized in 1972, offered small investors a way to pool their funds to invest in large denomination government securities and obtain higher interest earnings than were available through depository institutions. Commercial banks and thrifts soon felt their impact as depositors moved their funds to the highly popular money markets. A provision of the Garn St Germain Depository Institutions Act of 1982 now enables banks to compete with money market funds by offering a federally insured deposit account that pays interest determined at the sole discretion of the offering institution, but generally following a market-related rate. Money market funds remain strong competitors for commercial banks; however, many money market funds now also offer their customers checking, credit card, and borrowing services.

- *Securities brokerage firms,* such as Merrill Lynch, now package "cash management accounts" that provide money market funds and checking and credit services in conjunction with traditional securities trading services.

- *Major retailers* also offer an array of financial services through their subsidiaries. Sears customers, for example, can invest in money market funds or securities, as well as borrow, transfer funds, write checks, and purchase insurance.

Clearly, the public today has greater freedom of choice in selecting financial services from institutions other than commercial banks. A growing number of very differently regulated businesses are gaining the ability to offer a broader range of financial services by establishing or acquiring commercial banks or thrifts. Commercial banks and savings and loans are now owned through bank holding companies by mutual funds organizations, securities firms, insurance companies, and major retailers. Such moves are often accomplished by circumventing technical points of regulation. For example, acquisitions of savings and loans are allowed because there are no restrictions on holding companies that own a *single* savings and loan.[9] Acquisitions of banks have been possible because bank holding company regulations define a commercial bank as an institution that offers demand deposits *and* makes commercial loans; the bank holding company therefore acquires the bank and sells off the commerical loans.[10] A moratorium on such "limited purpose" banks was allowed to lapse on March 31, 1984 but has been reimposed by the Comptroller of the Currency until the end of the 1984 Congressional session.

It is clear that competitors are placing increasing pressure on commerical banks by continually looking for new ways to capture a share of the financial services market. Services that were once the sole province of banking have been opened up to competitors by changes in law and the development of innovative financial products. As a result, customers have become more sophisticated "shoppers"—aggressively seeking out financial products and services that more closely meet their needs and that offer the best price.

2
Bank Products and Services

Commercial banks link savers with borrowers by accepting deposits, extending credit, and making and collecting payments. In addition to these basic services, many banks offer specialized services, such as trust management, data processing, cash management, and financial consulting. Banks are also looking at new products and services that will generate fee income and service charges. An expanded line of financial products and services is essential for banks to satisfy customer demands, offset increased costs, and maintain profitability.

DEPOSIT SERVICES

The deposit services or products that banks offer include demand deposits, savings deposits, and time deposits. Deposits by bank customers are the major source of bank funds, although banks borrow funds from each other and from the Federal Reserve, and can sell stock to raise funds for additional capital.

- *Demand deposits* (checking accounts) are funds that can be withdrawn by customers on demand at any time. Checking account customers are primarily individuals, businesses, and government entities; they use demand deposits as a safe and convenient way to keep funds readily at hand to meet expenses. Traditionally, banks have not been allowed to offer interest on demand deposits, so, during periods of high interest rates, customers have kept their demand deposits to the minimum needed to cover their expected expenses. Today, commercial banks and other depository institutions are authorized to offer NOW (negotiable order of withdrawal) accounts that bear interest on deposits and provide checking services. Regular NOW accounts pay 5¼ percent interest on deposits. Super NOW accounts, which require a minimum balance of $2,500, allow unlimited transactions and pay interest at market rates.

- *Savings deposits* represent funds not needed now or in the near future that customers (primarily individuals) deposit for interest earnings. Savings deposits have no fixed maturity date. Before the phasing out of interest rate ceilings, thrift institutions were able to offer savings products that provided higher rates of interest than regular bank savings accounts. Today, banks are placing greater emphasis on providing attractive savings products because they recognize that customers want the added convenience, and that savings deposits (usually more stable over the long term than demand deposits) are an important source of bank funds.

- *Time deposits* are funds deposited for a specified time at a stated rate of interest that carry a penalty for early withdrawal before maturity. Time deposit products include certificates of deposit (CDs), money market certificates, money market accounts, Keogh and Individual Retirement Accounts (IRAs), and special savings club accounts.

  Certificates of deposit are the most popular form of time deposits and the largest single source of bank funds. CDs of $100,000 or more have no interest rate ceiling and are negotiable, providing easy transfer of ownership before maturity. Customers for negotiable CDs are individuals and large corporations.

  Money market certificates have a variety of maturities, and minimum denominations are set by individual banks. The interest paid on money market certificates is set by marketplace demands. Money market accounts, established in 1982, allow smaller depositors to obtain market rates on their funds. The minimum deposit for a money market account is $2,500, and this minimum must be maintained to receive market interest rates.

Keogh accounts and IRAs enable individuals to set aside tax deductible funds for retirement, with an exemption from taxes on principal and interest until withdrawal. Funds may not be withdrawn until age 59½ or until the depositor becomes disabled. Self-employed individuals can contribute up to 15% of their annual income (or $15,000 per year) to Keogh accounts; any individual may contribute up to $2,000 per year to an IRA if earned income is at least $2,000 a year.

Special savings club accounts allow customers to set funds aside regularly throughout the year for special purposes. The account balance and any interest earned is paid to the customer at the end of the specified savings period.

CREDIT SERVICES

Loans to individuals and businesses are the primary credit services offered by banks, and the largest source of bank income. (While bank investments in federal, state, and local government securities are actually indirect government loans, technically they are acquired assets, not marketable financial services that are sold to bank customers.) Bank credit services or products include commercial, consumer, real estate, and agricultural loans.

- *Commercial loans* represent the largest volume of credit services provided by banks. Such loans provide commercial and industrial businesses with funds to purchase raw materials and equipment, to pay salaries, and to expand their operations. Demand for business loans is cyclical and seasonal: when economic activity is high, businesses need more credit for production and employment, but as economic activity slows down, the demand for business credit eases; similarly, businesses need expanded credit to prepare for peak seasonal sales periods, after which the loans are repaid.

- *Consumer loans* are made to individuals for installment purchases of cars and other durable goods, for vacations, and for educational expenses. State laws set the maximum interest rates banks may charge for such loans, depending on the term of the loan and the type of purchase made. Bank credit cards, such as VISA and MasterCard, are also a widely used and rapidly growing form of consumer credit service.

- *Real estate loans* include residential mortgages, home construction, and home improvement loans. Residential mortgages traditionally have been offered by savings and loan associations, but as the demand for such loans has increased in recent years, commercial banks have recognized the potential for increased profits in this type of credit service. Today, commercial banks are the second largest holders of real estate mortgages.

- *Agricultural loans*, like business loans, enable farmers to purchase livestock, feed, and farm machinery and to pay other operating expenses. Such loans are concentrated in rural banks serving agricultural markets.

PAYMENT AND COLLECTION SERVICES

The payment and collection services provided by banks are a natural adjunct to bank deposit services. Checks are universally accepted in making payments and collections. Individuals and business customers rely on the safety, speed, and convenience of the banking system in processing payments and collections.

New payments and collection services have been developed using electronic funds transfer: information on deposits and withdrawals is recorded electronically and is instantly retrievable. Automated teller machines, preauthorized debiting of depositors' accounts, banking by phone, and point-of-sale terminals offer faster and more efficient forms of collection and payment at lower rates.

Large corporate customers use bank cash management services to accelerate their collection of funds and slow down their payments, so that they may have use of their funds for a longer period of time. Payments from a corporation's customers are made to a lock-box at a post office near the firm's bank, and these payments are collected frequently by bank personnel; cash receipts are immediately credited to the firm's account, and checks are quickly processed for collection. Often, total payments received are then transferred from the firm's collecting bank to its principal bank.

SPECIALIZED SERVICES

In addition to such familiar products as safe deposit boxes, traveler's checks, money orders, and cashier's checks, other specialized financial products provided by banks include trust services, data processing services, cash management information services, and financial consulting services.

- *Trust services* are provided by many banks on a fee basis to both individuals and businesses. Banks act as executors of the estates of deceased individuals, as trustees in managing the assets for beneficiaries named in trusts, and as agents on behalf of customers.

- *Data processing services* are provided by large banks that sell computer time and personnel capabilities for accounting purposes to small banks and other businesses. Such services generate profits that help banks offset the high cost of computers and staff.

- *Cash management services,* using computer technology, offer customers complete up-to-date data on the status of their accounts. Through their own computer terminals, businesses, correspondent banks, and government agencies can access bank computers to receive full daily printouts on the amounts and locations of balances and available funds in all accounts held by the customer. Such data can be supplemented with information on current possibilities for investments and funds transfers, thereby assisting the customer in financial decision-making. Customers can also make direct transfers of funds through the computer terminal. As the use of home computers becomes more common, cash management information services will become more readily available to individuals as well as corporate customers.

- *Financial consulting services* assist bank customers in decision-making on a variety of financial matters. Of course, individuals rely on banks for informal financial advice, and banks offer financial management advice to businesses that hold bank loans because the successful management of these businesses is the in the best interests of the lending banks. More formal financial consulting services may include advice on such matters as pricing business products, the best methods of raising business capital, and determining the appropriate rate of return on capital investments. Such services require staff expertise in specialized areas. In the near future, financial consulting services targeted at the retail customer will be an important product.

EXPANSION OF BANK PRODUCTS AND SERVICES

Several factors are contributing to the need for commercial banks to offer an expanded line of financial products and services. First, customers are demanding financial services that banks cannot provide under current law; as a result, bank customers are turning to other financial institutions not bound by regulatory constraints. Also, as noted earlier, bank customers are not only users of funds, but suppliers of funds as well. Banks "buy" most of the funds they use to extend credit by paying interest on customers' demand, savings, and time deposits.

Inflation, coupled with volatile interest rates, has increased the cost of securing and servicing customer deposits. Further, the deregulation of ceilings on the amount of interest that banks can pay for deposits, while allowing banks to compete for deposits at market rates, is increasing the cost of securing bank funds and reducing bank profitability. To satisfy customer demands, offset increased costs, and maintain profitability, banks are looking at new products and services that will generate service charges and fee income.

Many banks are examining the feasibility and profitability of new or expanded areas of financial service, such as securities underwriting, securities brokerage, mutual funds, commodities and futures brokerage, insurance underwriting, insurance brokerage, real estate brokerage, real estate equity, telecommunications, data processing, management consulting, and other services. Analysts are studying the attractiveness of these and other service markets in terms of their profit and growth potential, the ease of bank entry into these markets, and how well the new services or products would fit into existing bank services. Real estate equity, insurance brokerage, and discount securities brokerage appear to offer significant opportunities for expanded services by banks of all sizes, and full-service securities brokerage offers significant opportunities for mid-size and larger banks.[11]

3
Bank Organization and Technology

How do banks operate? To answer this question, we need to look at the nature of bank management, the basic functions of bank departments, the various approaches to departmental organization, and the technological changes that are altering the way banks do business.

BANK MANAGEMENT

The bank's stockholders elect the board of directors to represent them in seeing that the bank is well-managed, financially sound, profitable, competitive, market-oriented, and capable of future growth. The degree of actual participation by stockholders in management decisions varies with bank size; usually the larger the number of stockholders, the more removed they are from management decision-making.

The members of the board are legally responsible to the stockholders for directing the bank. The board elects the bank's president and other officers, establishes bank policies, supervises bank operations, and analyzes bank performance. It is the board's duty to see that management decisions are both prudent and legally sound. The board is accountable for bank results, and in some cases, personally liable for bank losses.

The chief executive officer carries out the board's policies by managing the bank's daily operations and monitoring the performance and profitability of each department in the bank. The bank's officers develop the specific strategies needed to carry out the board's policies; they coordinate departmental activities, train and develop staff, and continually review staff performance to ensure quality results. Because the bank's officers are closely involved with the details of daily operations and in direct contact with bank personnel, they are expected to recognize and propose needed changes in bank policy and strategy.

BASIC DEPARTMENTAL FUNCTIONS

In a small bank, an individual officer may carry out a wide range of duties. During a typical day, an officer might make a car loan, finance business equipment, hire a teller, plan an advertising campaign, and solicit a new business account. In a large bank, the greater volume of business and the more complex line of products and services necessitate the formation of separate departments for specialized functions. As we will see later, the organization and structure of departments within the bank can be approached in several different ways. While there is no standard organizational structure, some basic departmental functions are common to most banks that departmentalize their operations.

Loans

The credit function is the bank's main source of earnings income. The loan department is responsible for making individual and small business loans (consumer loans) and larger commercial loans (wholesale loans), and for loan servicing. Consumer lending services include installment loans, mortgages, and credit card operations. Wholesale lending services include short-term loans for business capital, long-term loans, and leases.

Deposits

The deposit function is the bank's main source of useable funds and represents a major part of the bank's expenses. This department services demand, savings, and time deposits for individual, small business, and corporate accounts. It also pays, collects, and processes checks, and handles money transfers between accounts.

Investments

The investment function is both a source of earnings and a source of liquidity for the bank. This department manages the bank's investment portfolio, handling the purchase and sale of federal, state, and local government securities. The department may coordinate the sale of large denomination certificates of deposit, the issue of repurchase agreements (long-term securities holdings sold with an agreement to rebuy before maturity), and the sale and purchase of Federal Funds (very short-term lending and borrowing between banks).

Trust

Because the trust function involves the custody and management of property in the interests of beneficiaries, the trust department must keep its assets separate from other bank assets.[12] The trust department provides services to corporations and individuals in the capacity of executor, trustee, or agent. It also acts as executor in settling individual estates; handles the management of corporate pension fund programs; acts as an agent for corporate stock transfers; and acts as trustee for corporate bondholders. The department takes custody of corporate securities and provides safekeeping, accounting, and tax services. Furthermore, it may be entrusted to make investment decisions regarding customer securities and, therefore, cannot have access to information generated by other departments of the bank that would influence investment decision-making.

Operations

Operations provides data processing and other support services to all other bank departments. As a broad category, operations includes accounting services, budget and performance analysis services, building and maintenance services, mail and delivery services, and security services. The cost of these operations is the bank's largest expense after interest expense and salaries and benefits.

Auditing

The auditing department provides the bank with a system of internal controls and regularly checks to see if control procedures are being followed. The department also sees that the bank is in compliance with industry regulations, working closely with regulatory agencies. The department checks the records of all the bank's accounts, and makes examinations of departments and branches. The auditing department reports directly to the board of directors, and usually the bank's auditor is directly appointed by the board.

Marketing

The marketing department coordinates the bank's public relations activities, conducts market research, and plans the bank's advertising. The department works closely with other departments that are in contact with customers to develop marketing strategies related to product development, pricing, promotion, and distribution. Often the bank's business development efforts are coordinated through the marketing department.

Personnel

The personnel or human resources department establishes staff policies and practices, and sees that the bank is in compliance with equal opportunity regulations. The department handles staff recruitment and hiring, establishes salaries, provides payroll services, and administers employee benefit programs.

In large banks, the personnel department also operates employee training programs. These internal training programs cover nearly all aspects of bank department functions, teaching employees basic job skills, correcting deficiencies in employee performance, keeping employees knowledgeable of industry changes, and preparing employees for career advancement. Most banks supplement such internal training by encouraging and supporting employee involvement in external training and education programs.

ORGANIZATIONAL METHODS

Most businesses of a similar nature have similar organizational structures, but this is not the case in banking. How a commercial bank is organized and structured depends on several variables: the size of the bank, its location and customer base, its branching environment, and in many cases, its connection with a bank holding company.

Size clearly affects the complexity of bank operations and organization. A few money center banks with assets of more than $20 billion are owned by thousands of stockholders; they do business worldwide through hundreds of branch offices, and they employ thousands of people. In contrast, many banks are small, privately owned businesses with assets under $25 million; their senior officers and board members may be the major stockholders, and their staffs may number less than two dozen employees.

Location and customer base determine the relative importance of functional service areas within a bank. If several banks serve the same location, some may focus their operations on either retail or commercial customers, emphasize one type of loan over another, or specialize in a specific type of financial service such as leasing or trusts. On the other hand, a bank serving a rural area often has a broader customer base, which requires a broader scope of services.

Branch administration is a major factor in organization and operations for banks in states that allow unlimited branching within a county, a region, or throughout the state. Likewise, whether or not a bank is connected with a bank holding company affects bank organization and operations. Functional lines of authority differ with state laws and the nature of the bank's relationship with the holding company. Banks owned by holding companies typically have their own boards of directors who may retain substantial autonomy in establishing local bank policy. In some cases, the management of the holding company and the management of the predominant bank owned by the company may be one and the same.

As a result of these variables, the departmentalization of specific services within a bank takes various forms. It is managaement's responsibility to determine what departments should be formed to meet customer needs most effectively and to assure bank efficiency. As we have seen, departments may be structured by function; they may also be structured by type of customer served, by product type, by geographic location, or by a combination of these methods.

Figure 1 shows a mixed approach to departmentalization; that is, several approaches are combined. First, the functional approach is the basis of the organizational structure in that the major departments are formed according to the types of activities carried out. Many smaller banks that departmentalize follow this approach. Department organization by customer type is also shown in Figure 1 by the retail and commercial divisions of the marketing department. Many banks use the customer approach to combine different service functions based on market served, forming consumer and wholesale departments that handle both deposit and loan services for their respective markets. Figure 1 shows product departmentalization by the division of the loan department into consumer, commercial, real estate, and agricultural loans. In large banks, this form of organization reflects the need for staff who are product specialists. Geographical departmentalization is

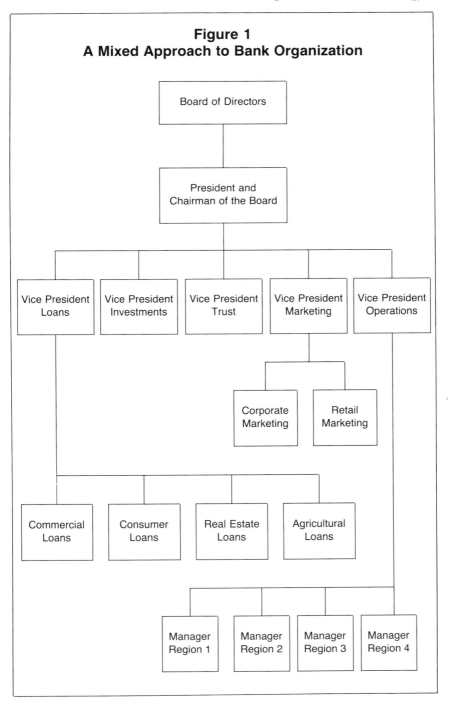

Figure 1
A Mixed Approach to Bank Organization

used in banks involved in branching, particularly banks that may branch statewide. This form of organization is shown by the division of operations into four regional departments. The organizational structure shown in Figure 1 is only one of several possible strategies for departmental organization. Each bank must choose the organizational approach that best reflects its individual characteristics and its business objectives.

BANK TECHNOLOGY

Bank operations develop and change as a bank's volume of business increases and as the bank expands its line of products and services. Advances in technology are also causing changes in the way many banks operate.

Most notably, technology is bringing greater cost efficiency to banking. Banks now can service their customers with automated teller machines (ATMs) at many locations, thereby reducing the cost of building and maintaining large facilities. Greater efficiency and reduced cost in the check transfer payment system are possible through the use of automated clearinghouses, electronic funds transfer systems, and check truncation (the storage of checks where received, eliminating physical transfer).

Technology is also providing the means for banks to offer an expanded line of services at lower costs to the customer. Advances in data processing give greater economy to joint production and distribution—a single financial firm may be able to produce two different types of financial services together for less cost than two firms operating separately.

Another result of technology is increased competition among banks. Advances in the field of communications are changing customer accessibility to national money and capital markets. With today's communications systems, customers in the smallest communities can invest in assets that earn national market rates.

As more banks make use of existing technology, and as new technologies are developed, bank department functions and operations will continue to change to provide better services for customers and greater cost efficiency for banks.

4

Bank Profitability

In banking, as in any business, profitability is essential for survival and growth. Bank stockholders expect an adequate return on their investments; if bank profits are weak, stockholders will place future investment funds elsewhere. Profitability also encourages investors to provide the additional capital needed for new bank products and services. In addition, profitability is a measure of the bank's effectiveness in serving the needs of the public: banks must be competitive to assure profitability. Today, bank customers are demanding more and varied financial products and services. In order to stay competitive and retain profits, banks must be able to expand their operations to meet this demand.

Because bank customers are both suppliers and users of bank funds, certain factors that affect customer behavior—inflation and fluctuating interest rates—are also increasing the costs to banks of securing and servicing customer deposits. Interest rate volatility is increasing the demand for short-term assets over long-term assets. The deregulation of interest rate ceilings on deposits is also increasing the relative costs of funds and may reduce banks' net interest margins.

To offset increased costs and maintain profitability, banks are finding that they must generate new income through fees and service charges for many of their financial products and services. The ability to offer a wider range of financial products and services will make banks less vulnerable to fluctuating interest rates, will check declining profitability by providing increased income from fees and service charges, and will enable banks to meet the needs and demands of their customers.

Basically, profitability depends on a bank's ability to serve two markets: depositors want to be paid the highest available rate for supplying funds, and borrowers want to pay the lowest possible rate for using funds. To earn an adequate return for its stockholders, the bank must create a "spread" between the amount it pays for funds and the amount it charges for funds.

The bank's sources of funds (deposits) are its *liabilities;* the bank's uses of funds (loans and investments) are its *assets.*

Bankers traditionally focused their attention on managing assets because they could count on a stable flow of deposits into checking accounts and low-interest savings accounts. In the mid-1960s, however, increased competition for customer deposits from other depository institutions forced banks to focus on the active management of their liabilities, and as a result, new deposit products were created.

With the wide fluctuation of interest rates in the 1970s, bankers found they had to focus on yet another area of funds management: the relationship between interest-rate-sensitive assets and interest-rate-sensitive liabilities. This is the basis of today's asset/liability management.

The bank's effectiveness in managing its assets and liabilities is shown by examining the bank's financial statements—the balance sheet and the income statement.

The Balance Sheet

A balance sheet is a statement of a bank's financial condition that lists the bank's assets and liabilities as of a specified date. Again, assets represent the bank's uses of funds; liabilities represent the bank's sources of funds. Since banks do not produce tangible goods or maintain inventories, some balance sheet items or their placement may need clarification. Exhibit 1 shows a sample balance sheet. A description of typical balance sheet items follows.

Exhibit 1
A Typical Balance Sheet

```
        STATEMENT OF CONDITION
             May 31, 19XX
```

	(in hundreds)
ASSETS:	
EARNING ASSETS	
Deposits with Banks	xxx,xxx
LOANS	
Real Estate-Construction	x,xxx,xxx
Real Estate-Mortgage	xx,xxx,xxx
Commercial/Industrial	x,xxx,xxx
Agribusiness	x,xxx,xxx
Individual/Personal	x,xxx,xxx
All Other Loans	x,xxx,xxx
Lease Financing	-0-
TOTAL LOANS	xx,xxx,xxx
INVESTMENT SECURITIES	
U.S. Treasury	x,xxx,xxx
State and Municipal	x,xxx,xxx
Other Securities	xxx,xxx
TOTAL INVESTMENT SECURITIES	x,xxx,xxx
TRADING ACCOUNT SECURITIES	
Federal Funds Sold	xxx,xxx
TOTAL EARNING ASSETS	xx,xxx,xxx
Allowance for Loan Losses	xxx,xxx
TOTAL EARNING ASSETS AFTER ALLOWANCE	xx,xxx,xxx
NON-EARNING ASSETS	
Cash and Due From Banks	x,xxx,xxx
PREMISES & EQUIPMENT	
Land	xx,xxx
Buildings	xxx,xxx
Leasehold Improvements	-0-
Furniture and equipment	xxx,xxx
TOTAL PREMISES AND EQUIPMENT	
Accrued Income Receivable	xxx,xxx
Miscellaneous Other Assets	xxx,xxx

Exhibit 1 continued

	(in hundreds)
TOTAL NON-EARNING ASSETS	x,xxx,xxx
TOTAL ASSETS	xx,xxx,xxx
LIABILITIES:	
INTEREST BEARING LIABILITIES	
Savings & Time Deposits	
Savings	x,xxx,xxx
NOW Accounts (Regular)	x,xxx,xxx
Money Rate Checking	x,xxx,xxx
Personal Money Market	x,xxx,xxx
Business Money Market	x,xxx,xxx
Other Time Deposits	xx,xxx,xxx
TOTAL TIME AND SAVINGS	xx,xxx,xxx
BORROWED FUNDS	
Federal Funds Purchased/Securities Sold	xxx,xxx
Borrowed Funds	xx,xxx
Capital Notes/Debentures	-0-
TOTAL BORROWED FUNDS	xxx,xxx
TOTAL INTEREST BEARING LIABILITIES	xx,xxx,xxx
NON-INTEREST BEARING LIABILITIES	
Demand Deposits	x,xxx,xxx
Accrued Income Taxes	x,xxx
Accrued Expenses	xxx,xxx
Dividends Declared	xx,xxx
Other Miscellaneous Liabilities	xx,xxx
TOTAL NON-INTEREST BEARING LIABILITIES	x,xxx,xxx
TOTAL LIABILITIES	xx,xxx,xxx
SHAREHOLDERS EQUITY	
Capital	xxx,xxx
Surplus	xxx,xxx
Undivided Profits	x,xxx,xxx
Treasury Stock	-0-
TOTAL SHAREHOLDERS EQUITY	x,xxx,xxx
TOTAL LIABILITIES/SHAREHOLDERS EQUITY	xx,xxx,xxx

Assets

Assets are what the bank owns. The types of assets listed are fairly consistent from bank to bank because they are highly regulated.

- *Cash and Due From Banks* refers to a bank's primary reserves—what is in the bank's vault or on deposit with another bank. This account may be the sum of four separate assets: working cash, reserves, balances at respondent banks, and uncollected cash items.

  First, working cash must be held in reserve to meet day-to-day operating expenses, and to serve customer needs for check cashing and loans.

  Second, the Federal Reserve requires all depository institutions to hold a percentage of their deposits in reserves. The usual reserve requirement is from 3 percent to 12 percent, and it varies with the type of account and the size of the institution. In some cases, the Fed can raise the reserve requirements for transaction accounts. Reserves may be held as vault cash or in an account at a Federal Reserve Bank.

  A third part of a bank's primary reserves may include balances in accounts held at another bank with whom the bank has a correspondent relationship. A large correspondent bank may assist a smaller respondent bank by allowing it to participate in making loans that would otherwise be beyond the assets of the smaller bank. Balances in accounts held at the smaller respondent bank are assets of the larger correspondent bank.

  Fourth, cash items in the process of collection are a large part of this category. These items (primarily checks) have been credited to customers' accounts, but the money has not yet been received from other banks (this is called *float*).

  The bank's primary reserves are held to a minimum because they cannot be used to meet liquidity needs and because these assets earn no income. Excess working cash and correspondent balances can be invested in short-term securities or Federal Funds. This provides income for the bank. Furthermore, as short-term investments, they can easily be converted into cash if necessary.

- *Investment Securities* refers to securities purchased by banks to provide liquidity, income, and collateral.

  Investments that can be easily converted into cash to meet liquidity needs are known as "secondary reserves." Short-term U.S. government securities, Treasury bills, and commercial paper are most frequently held for this purpose. There is no standard formula for determining how much should be held in secondary reserves, although loan and deposit demands are a major consideration. The objective is to meet unexpected loan demands or deposit withdrawals without undue reliance on borrowing or the sacrifice of investment income.

  The "investment account" refers to securities not included in the secondary reserves. Securities in the investment account are of longer-term maturity than secondary reserves and are purchased for their income rather than their liquidity. The investment account contains credit risk and interest rate risk.

  Banks are limited by regulatory agencies in the types of investments they may purchase.[13] Board members should receive periodic reports on the investment portfolio to examine the quality, diversification, and maturities of the investment securities held.

- *Federal Funds Sold* represents a temporary short-term transfer of excess reserves to another bank that has a need for the funds. Banks regularly buy and sell Federal Funds as their needs dictate. Federal Funds Sold is a loan and, as such, draws interest.

- *Loans Outstanding* usually represents the bank's largest asset. Interest on loans is a major source of income for the bank. Some balance sheets show figures for gross loans and net loans (gross loans less a reserve allowance for estimated loan losses).

  Making loans is a part of the bank's responsibility to the community and a basic function of the bank's role as financial intermediary. The size and composition of the bank's loan portfolio are influenced by the needs and demands of the community. A standard or typical amount outstanding in the loan portfolio cannot be recommended for all banks. A general rule of thumb, though, is that the higher the loan-to-deposit ratio, the greater the amount of bank credit that is being extended.

The sample balance sheet shows loans broken down by type because types of credit vary with local demand and different loan products have different yields and maturities. Although there are few restrictions on the types of loans a commercial bank can make, bank lending is closely governed by laws and regulations. For example, banks are restricted on the size of real estate portfolios,[14] the amount of credit extended for purchasing stock, and the collateral they may accept. Loans to bank officers, directors, affiliates, and bank holding companies are also regulated.

Another important restriction relates to the amount of credit that a bank can extend to one borrower.[15] This is commonly referred to as the bank's legal lending limit. Generally, the maximum allowable to one borrower is 15 percent of the bank's capital and surplus accounts. However, depending on federal or state regulation, there are a number of exceptions to the rule. Violation of the legal lending limit creates an illegal loan situation and possible personal liability for a director.

- *Bank Premises and Equipment* represents the bank's least liquid assets. The bank's premises should create an image of substance, durability, and success without an inordinate investment of capital assets. Expansion of branch offices, modernization of facilities, and automation have increased the size of this account in recent years.

- *Other Assets* is a catch-all category, generally made up of prepaid expenses.

Liabilities

Liabilities are what the bank owes, and reflect the bank's heavy dependence on the use of borrowed funds.

- *Total Deposits* represents the main source of bank funds and the largest share of the bank's liabilities. Deposits are classified as demand, savings, and time deposits. Until the mid-1960s, the dollar volume of demand deposits exceeded time and savings deposits. But, as the public became more sensitive to higher interest rates, and as banks aggressively sought funds by offering competitive deposit products, the volume of time and savings deposits surpassed demand deposits.

- Liabilities other than deposits include: *Federal Funds Purchased* (short-term borrowing of excess funds from other banks); *Other Borrowed Funds* (borrowing from the Federal Reserve or through repurchase agreements); *Accrued Taxes and Interest* (the amount set aside to pay taxes and interest on deposits); and *Other Liabilities* (taxes payable, salaries payable, accounts payable, and dividends payable).

Capital Accounts

Capital accounts are what the bank owes its owners. Capital accounts are commonly referred to as shareholders equity.

- *Capital Notes* (or *Debentures*) represents obligations that are not backed by collateral but are sold on the integrity of the bank. A bank must first honor depositors' claims, then capital notes, then stockholders' claims. To raise capital, some banks prefer to issue capital notes or debentures rather than issue more stock. Each option has advantages and disadvantages due to such variables as marketability, tax position, and future earnings.

- *Common Stock* shows the total par value of shares purchased by investors (par value per share multiplied by the number of shares sold). Most banks issue only common stock.

- *Surplus* represents two sources of funds: funds paid by stockholders in excess of the par value of an initital stock issue, and retained earnings.

- *Undivided Earnings* represents stockholders' earnings from operations that are not paid out as dividends or allocated elsewhere.

THE INCOME STATEMENT

The income statement is a report of the operating income and expenses of the bank over a specified period of time (usually a month, quarter, or year). The income statement shows the bank's profits or losses. Exhibit 2 shows a typical income statement. A description of some of the major items found on an income statement follows.

Revenues

The major source of bank revenue is interest and fees on loans, followed by interest earned on all investments. Additional revenues include trust department income, service charges on accounts, commissions and fees, and other operating income. Banks are placing more emphasis on fee income as a source of revenue because of increased competition from other financial institutions for customer deposits and because of the growing cost of interest that must be paid on deposits.

Expenses

As noted earlier, interest paid on deposits now surpasses wages and salaries as the bank's largest area of expense. Additional expenses include assessments for FDIC insurance, and other operating costs such as advertising, printing, and office supplies.

Exhibit 2
A Typical Income Statement

STATEMENT OF INCOME AND EXPENSE
TAX EQUIVALENT*
May 31, 1984 Year-to-Date

(in hundreds)

INTEREST INCOME
INTEREST DEPOSITS WITH BANK
INTEREST AND FEES ON LOANS

Real Estate-Construction	xx,xxx
Real Estate-Mortgage	xxx,xxx
Financial Institutions	-0-
Purchasing/Carring Securities	-0-
Agribusiness	xxx,xxx
Commercial/Industrial	xxx,xxx
Individual/Personal	xxx,xxx
All Other Loans	xx,xxx
Lease Financing	-0-
TOTAL INTEREST AND FEES ON LOANS	x,xxx,xxx

INTEREST/DIVIDENDS ON SECURITIES

U.S. Treasury	xxx,xxx
State/Municipal	xxx,xxx
U.S. Agencies	-0-
Other Securities	-0-
TOTAL INTEREST AND DIVIDENDS ON SECURITIES	xxx,xxx

INTEREST/DIVIDENDS ON TRADING SECURITIES

Interest on Federal Funds Sold	-0-
TOTAL INTEREST INCOME	x,xxx,xxx

INTEREST EXPENSE
INTEREST ON DEPOSITS

NOW Accounts	xxx,xxx
Savings Deposits	xx,xxx
Money Market	xxx,xxx
Other Time Deposits	xxx,xxx
TOTAL INTEREST ON DEPOSITS	x,xxx,xxx

INTEREST ON BORROWED FUNDS

Federal Funds Purchased/Sold	-0-
Borrowed Funds	-0-
Capital Notes	-0-
TOTAL INTEREST ON BORROWED FUNDS	-0-

Exhibit 2 continued

	(in hundreds)
TOTAL INTEREST EXPENSE	x,xxx,xxx
INTEREST MARGIN BEFORE PROVISION	x,xxx,xxx
Provision for Losses	xxx,xxx
INTEREST MARGIN AFTER PROVISION	xxx,xxx
NON-INTEREST INCOME	
Trading Accounts	-0-
Services Charges on NOW Accounts	-0-
Services Charges on Deposit Accounts	xx,xxx
Trust Department Income	-0-
Credit Card Income	xx,xxx
Other Service Charges	xx,xxx
Leasing Income-Operating Leases	-0-
Securities Gains (Losses)	-0-
Other Income	xx,xxx
TOTAL NON-INTEREST INCOME	xxx,xxx
NON-INTEREST EXPENSE	
SALARIES AND BENEFITS	
Salaries - Officers	xxx,xxx
Salaries - Employees	xxx,xxx
Employee Benefits	xx,xxx
TOTAL SALARIES AND BENEFITS	xxx,xxx
OCCUPANCY EXPENSE	
Building Depreciation	x,xxx
Amortized Leasehold Improvements	-0-
Rent Expense	xx,xxx
Occupancy Expense	xx,xxx
Rental Income - Tenants	-0-
TOTAL OCCUPANCY EXPENSE	xx,xxx
GENERAL EXPENSE	
Marketing	xx,xxx
Computer Service	xx,xxx
Equipment Expense	xx,xxx
Depreciation Furniture and Equipment	xx,xxx
Personal Property Tax	x,xxx
Director's Fees	x,xxx
Donations	x,xxx

Exhibit 2 continued

	(in hundreds)
Examination Assessment	x,xxx
Federal Deposit Insurance	xx,xxx
Insurance - Other	x,xxx
Legal and Professional	x,xxx
Dues, Education, Subscriptions	x,xxx
Postage and Delivery	xx,xxx
Printing, Stationery, Supplies	xx,xxx
Telephone	x,xxx
Travel and Entertainment	xx,xxx
Credit Card Expenses	xx,xxx
Depreciation - Operating Leases	-0-
Other Expense	xx,xxx
TOTAL GENERAL EXPENSE	xxx,xxx
TOTAL NON-INTEREST EXPENSE	xxx,xxx
NET NON-INTEREST EXPENSE	xxx,xxx
INCOME BEFORE TAXES	xxx,xxx
PROVISION FOR INCOME TAXES	
Provision for Income Tax	xx,xxx
Tax Equivalent Income Tax	xxx,xxx
TOTAL PROVISION FOR INCOME TAX	xxx,xxx
NET INCOME	xxx,xxx
NET SECURITIES GAINS/LOSSES	-0-
TAX EFFECT SECURITIES GAINS/LOSSES	-0-
TOTAL NET SECURITIES GAINS/LOSSES	-0-
NET INCOME AFTER SECURITIES GAINS/LOSSES	xxx,xxx
DIVIDENDS	xxx,xxx
INCOME AFTER DIVIDENDS	xx,xxx

*Tax Equivalent—means that the tax-free investments (state and municipal investments) have been adjusted up to reflect the tax exempt effect and this effect has been adjusted in the tax equivalent income tax section of the provision for income tax area of the statement.

Net Income

Gross expenses subtracted from gross income shows the bank's net income (profit or loss). Strong profits are needed to pay dividends to stockholders, to offset loan losses, to pay ongoing operating expenses, to retain earnings to build stockholder equity, and for future expansion of products and services.

MEASURES OF PROFITABILITY

In banking, there are two measures of profitability that give a better picture of bank performance than dollar profits alone: return on equity and return on assets.

- *Return on equity* shows the relationship between profits and the stockholders' investment, and tells how efficiently equity capital is invested. Return on equity is calculated by relating yearly net income (gross income minus taxes and securities gains or losses) to average equity:

$$ROE = \frac{net\ income}{average\ equity}$$

- *Return on assets* shows the relationship between profits and assets, and tells how efficiently assets are used. Return on assets is calculated by relating yearly net income to average total assets:

$$ROA = \frac{net\ income}{average\ total\ assets}$$

Return on assets is an important measure of bank performance because a bank's profitability may decline, even though its earnings are growing, if assets are not put to good use.

The use of profitability ratios to measure bank performance is discussed further in Chapter 8.

5

Bank Regulation

The regulation of the financial services industry has changed significantly in the last few years. For one thing, the Federal Reserve has assumed greater power over monetary policy by subjecting all depository institutions to its reserve requirements. In return, Federal Reserve services are now available to all depository institutions, and explicit pricing of Fed services is being implemented. And perhaps most significantly, interest rate ceilings on savings deposits are being phased out, and the differential that allowed thrifts to pay higher rates on savings deposits has been eliminated. Nevertheless, banks still remain highly restricted in terms of the *prices* they can charge for credit products, the *procedures* they must follow, the *places* where they can do business, and the *products* they can offer.

Banking has long been one of the most closely regulated of all industries because it deals in a public commodity and because its operations are so important to the national economy. Banks are regulated by both state and federal government agencies, and bankers often refer to this as the "dual system" of regulation. Regulation involves the approval of bank charters, the formation of rules governing industry operations, and the supervision and enforcement of those rules through bank monitoring and examination.

The purpose of government regulation of banking is fourfold:

- to assure the safety and soundness of the banking system;
- to protect bank customers;

43

- to protect bank owners against management fraud and provide them with reasonable returns on their investments; and

- to promote competition within the industry.

To achieve these goals, regulations have been developed covering many areas, including the terms and conditions for obtaining and using funds. Moreover, bank branching, mergers, and acquisitions are restricted to keep the industry competitive by preventing the consolidation of many small banks into industry giants. To control competition, the types of business a bank may enter are restricted. Bank customers are protected by regulations that insure deposits against loss, prohibit consumer discrimination, and set forth customers' rights. Regulations on required capital and guidelines on liquidity, solvency, and profitability protect the investments of bank stockholders.

REGULATORY AUTHORITIES

As shown in Table 2, banks can be classified into four groups based on their relationships to regulatory authorities. An overlapping of authority is inevitable, but regulatory duties are divided among authorities so that overlapping is minimized.

All banks must be chartered. A charter application requires substantial information about the bank's organizers and the adequacy of the proposed bank's capital structure. Market research must also support the need for a new bank in the community. A charter is granted only when it is evident that the proposed bank is needed and that it can operate in a safe and profitable manner.

For a national charter, the chartering agency is the Office of the Comptroller of the Currency; for a state charter, it is a state banking agency. The choice of charter determines whether a bank is classified as a national bank or a state bank.

National banks must be members of the Federal Reserve System and insured by the Federal Deposit Insurance Corporation. Federal Reserve membership is optional for state banks, but requires insurance by the FDIC. Nonmember banks have the option of FDIC insurance.

Table 2
Categories of Commercial
Banks

Type of Bank	Regulatory Authority
National bank	Office of the Comptroller of the Currency (OCC)
	Federal Reserve System
	Federal Deposit Insurance Corporation (FDIC)
State member* bank	State banking authorities
	Federal Reserve System
	FDIC
State nonmember, FDIC-insured bank	State banking authorities
	FDIC
State nonmember, non-FDIC insured bank	State banking authorities

*The term *member* or *nonmember* refers to membership in the Federal Reserve System

Office of the Comptroller of the Currency

The Office of the Comptroller of the Currency (OCC) is a bureau of the Treasury Department and is responsible for issuing and overseeing national charters. It also makes a thorough examination of all the affairs of each national bank on a regular basis.[16] The scope of the examination can vary, and three types of examinations are performed: general, specialized, and special supervisory. There are about 4,500 national banks regulated by the OCC.

Federal Reserve System

The Federal Reserve System consists of 12 district banks with 25 branches, and is coordinated by the Board of Governors in Washington, D.C. Fewer than 6,000 banks are members of the Federal Reserve System, with only about 1,000 of the more than 9,600 state-chartered banks having chosen to become members. Fed member banks control nearly 80 percent of all U.S. bank deposits, however, and this gives the Federal Reserve a commanding influence over the nation's money supply.

Some of the Fed's main supervisory powers include the power to enforce consumer protection rules, to receive state banks into the Federal Reserve System, to approve the establishment of bank holding companies, and to examine and regulate BHCs' operations.

In terms of general monetary policy, the Fed's *open market operations* are most often used to stimulate or slow down the economy. When the economy needs stimulating, the Fed buys government or nongovernment securities on the open market. The money it spends flows into the sellers' checking accounts and can be used by banks for loans and investments. When the Fed sells securities, they are paid for by money in the buyers' checking accounts. The money supply contracts, interest rates begin to rise, and, with time, the economy slows down.

The Fed has two other tools it uses to keep the economy healthy and growing: *reserve requirements* and the *discount rate.*

As noted earlier, the Fed now requires all depository institutions to keep a certain percentage of their deposits in reserve.[17] These reserves are set aside in cash in the bank's vault and in a reserve account at the Federal Reserve Bank. The percentage of reserves required depends on the size and location of the institution and the classification of the deposits. Changing the legal reserve requirements increases or decreases the amount of money banks have to lend or invest, thereby affecting the level of the money supply.

Second, the Fed controls the discount rate, which is the interest rate a bank pays when it needs to borrow from the Fed. By raising the discount rate, the Fed makes it more costly for banks to borrow and this, in turn, increases the cost of borrowing for bank customers. Lowering the discount rate allows banks to lend more money at lower rates, thereby increasing borrowing by bank customers.

Borrowing at the discount rate is one method of adjusting a bank's reserve position, with credit generally extended to a bank on a short-term basis. Access to this Fed *discount window* was previously a privilege of Fed membership, but the Depository Institutions Deregulation and Monetary Control Act of 1980 changed this by allowing all depository institutions to borrow from the Fed, which they usually only do when they cannot borrow funds elsewhere. Borrowed funds must be fully collateralized by U.S. government securities or eligible paper.

Federal Deposit Insurance Corporation

The FDIC, created in 1933, insures each bank depositor's account for up to $100,000 in the event of bank failure. All national banks must carry FDIC insurance, and all but a few state-chartered banks do so by choice or to comply with state laws. Banks are assessed a percentage of their deposits for the insurance coverage.[18]

In case a bank encounters financial difficulty, the FDIC may move in one of three ways:

- *Pay depositors the amount of their insured deposits.*[19] The FDIC then acts as a receiver in settling the bank's affairs if so requested by the Comptroller of the Currency or the state banking administrator.

- *Strengthen the bank by lending money to, buying assets from, or making deposits in the bank.*[20] This action could be taken when the bank's closing would seriously hamper the functioning of the community.

- *Help the troubled bank merge or consolidate with a sound bank.*[21] To merge means that one bank loses its corporate identity and its assets are combined with another bank's assets. A consolidation occurs when two or more banks combine to form a new bank. The FDIC also has examination authority over all banks insured by them.

State Banking Authorities

State banks are chartered, regulated, and supervised by state banking commissioners or supervisors. These authorities frequently examine state banks to determine if the banks are financially sound and in compliance with state laws and regulations. State authorities also rule on applications for acquisitions and branching. Under the McFadden Act of 1927, national banks are restricted from branching unless branching is permitted by state law.[22] Thus, although the federal government charters national banks, the individual states decide if national banks and all other banks located in the state may open branch offices.

REGULATORY FUNCTIONS

There is a degree of overlap of federal and state authority, but the agencies have delineated areas of responsibility, and they coordinate efforts in bank examinations to minimize duplication. The functions of the federal and state authorities vary somewhat, but their central purpose is to maintain a sound banking system.

Other functions of state or federal supervisors include—

- *Issuing regulations, rulings, and instructions.* Guidelines reflecting changes in policies and procedures are distributed to banks for their information and compliance.

- *Compiling statistical reports and data.* This includes comparative information on bank performance measures.

- *Protecting depositors' funds.* Banks are required to file periodic reports with various agencies. Through examinations and reported information, the agencies determine the bank's solvency, competency of management, and any violations of law or of sound banking practices. Corrective measures can then be recommended or imposed before serious trouble occurs.[23]

THE MONETARY CONTROL ACT

The Depository Institutions Deregulation and Monetary Control Act of 1980 (commonly called the Monetary

Control Act) made the most significant changes in banking law since the 1930s. The act expanded the powers of the Federal Reserve and increased its control over monetary policy, changed the competitive relationship between banks and thrifts, provided consumers with opportunities for higher interest earnings, and authorized banks to offer new interest-earning transaction accounts. Specifically, the act[24]—

- subjected all depository institutions to the Fed's reserve requirements;

- created the Depository Institutions Deregulation Committee (DIDC) to supervise the gradual phaseout of interest rate ceilings on time and savings deposits at banks and thrifts;

- authorized all depository institutions to offer NOW accounts, make automatic funds transfers, and operate remote service units;

- gave broader lending powers to federal savings and loans and federal mutual savings banks;

- increased federal deposit insurance to $100,000; and

- required the explicit pricing of Federal Reserve Bank services.

These and other provisions are causing important changes in the financial services industry. The Federal Reserve now has greater control over monetary policy because virtually all depository institutions are subject to its reserve requirements. Prior to the act, thrifts were allowed to pay higher interest rates on time and savings deposits than commercial banks. The phasing out both of this differential and of interest rate ceilings on time and savings deposits is increasing competition between thrifts and commercial banks. Competition is also intensifying because of the new ability of all depository institutions to offer popular NOW accounts and other new services. Explicit pricing of Fed services is forcing banks to make their operations more cost-effective and to depend more on each other for services (providing greater opportunities for correspondent banks).

These changes are healthy because they enhance the competitive environment. Further proposals, now before Congress, for restructuring the regulation of the financial services industry may provide equally dramatic changes as time goes on.

BANK RESTRICTIONS AND REGULATORY REFORM

In the last decade, market rates soared above the interest rate ceilings on deposits imposed by regulatory agencies on banks and other depository institutions. Banks and thrifts felt the effects of the resulting *disintermediation* as customers moved their funds into highly liquid market rate deposit instruments such as money market funds. The Monetary Control Act of 1980 attempted to counter this disintermediation by appointing the DIDC to gradually phase out all interest rate ceilings on deposits. The DIDC created some shorter-term deposit products offering market rates, but its primary focus was on eliminating ceilings on long-term deposits, and banks and thrifts continued to feel the effects of disintermediation.

In 1982, the Garn St Germain Depository Institutions Act authorized the money market deposit account to enable banks to compete with money market funds.[25] Soon after, the Super NOW account was created, and banks are now better able to compete in the marketplace for customer deposits. Despite these advances, reform is still needed in the regulations that restrict bank *pricing, procedures, place,* and *products.*

Banks continue to be restricted in the prices they charge for credit (usury ceilings). Studies show that such restrictions on lending, while designed to benefit the consumer, may, in fact, be counterproductive: credit may be provided only to the lowest-risk customers, thus stifling the economy; small, low-rate loans may be eliminated; prices of goods and services may be higher in states with restricted lending ceilings; and some consumers may be forced to pay more for credit elsewhere.[26] The elimination or liberalization of usury ceilings would enable banks to provide better service to credit customers.

Restrictions on procedures must also be considered in future regulatory reform. Banks are now faced with a prodigious number of consumer protection laws that require the compilation and disclosure of increasing amounts of data. Such regulations are reducing bank efficiency and productivity, and studies show that consumers make little use of the information made available to them.[27]

Reform is also needed in regulations that determine where banks may do business. The geographic distribution of banks is governed by state authorities rather than the federal government, but savings and loans and nonbank institutions are less restricted, and their movement across state lines has become widespread.[28] This inequity must be corrected.

Finally, and most importantly, future regulatory changes must recognize the need for banks to offer a broader range of financial products and services. The 98th Congress is currently considering the Financial Institutions Deregulation Act and the Depository Institutions Holding Company Act Amendments of 1983[29] that offer great potential for the expansion of bank products and services, the simplification of bank regulations, and a more equitable form of regulation for all financial institutions. Four basic principles underlie these proposals:

- The types of products and services that can be offered by commercial banks should be expanded.

- The process for gaining regulatory approval of banks entering many of the permitted service areas should be simplified.

- The same regulatory restrictions should be imposed on all firms supplying the same service (functional regulation).

- All new activities should be segregated in a subsidiary of a bank holding company. (The legislation would allow an exception to this principle for securities services in banks below a certain size.)

This proposal would allow banks to serve their customers more effectively by expanding the range of products and services they can offer to include insurance brokerage and underwriting, real estate investments, real estate development and brokerage, underwriting state and local revenue bonds (except certain industrial development bonds), and mutual fund services. In addition, the proposal directs the Federal Reserve to expand the list of allowed activities to include *any business of a financial nature.* This aspect of the proposal would greatly enhance the ability of commercial banks to meet evolving customer needs in the future. The freedom to offer new products and services and the simplified process of regulatory approval for banks entering newly approved service areas would also enhance the competitive environment.

The principle of functional regulation (imposing the same regulatory restrictions on all firms supplying the same services) would ensure bank viability and profitability, regardless of bank size, because all financial institutions would compete under the same rules. And, by placing new services in subsidiaries of bank holding companies, banks would be insulated from any risk associated with new services, thereby protecting the safety and soundness of the banking system.

Regulatory restructuring of the financial services industry must continue in order for banks to provide their customers with needed financial products and services at reasonable costs.

6

Implications of Industry Trends for Directors

The American commercial banking industry is a unique system that has been shaped by the nation's periods of economic panic, failure, and success. Recent regulatory changes have been significant, and changes in the system are again on the horizon through pending legislation. Today's bank directors will be actively involved in shaping the future of commercial banking. Those who serve on bank boards will consider bank participation in a number of challenging areas—changing technologies, increased competition, new services, and regulatory reform, to name a few.

This book provides an overview of the knowledge and skills needed for competency as a bank director, but the business of banking is developing and expanding rapidly. The complexity of banking today requires that bank directors have extensive information so that they can fulfill their responsibilities in setting and overseeing bank policies and in guiding and evaluating bank management. Bankers, regulators, and legislators will play critical roles in deciding the course of our banking and monetary systems. Keeping up-to-date on competitive trends, technology, legislation, new services, and personalities in banking today will help directors focus on the key issues.

Banks are facing increasing competitive pressures resulting from changes in law and the introduction of new financial products, and directors must see that banks offer quality products and services at competitive rates to hold customer business. Banks are also facing increasing costs in securing and servicing customer deposits, and directors must see that banks attempt to expand their product lines to generate service charges and fee income. Technological advances are bringing greater efficiency and reduced cost in bank operations, and directors must see that banks take advantage of such developments. It is especially vital that board members be familiar with pending legislation and its potential impact on the banking industry, and that they are prepared to take proper action. Finally, there is a growing trend toward strict enforcement of the laws concerning bank directors. Banking is becoming more complex, and directors bear greater responsibilities than ever before. Directors are being held more strictly accountable for bank performance, an indication of which is the growing number of actions by stockholders against directors.

The times dictate the need for all directors to make planning a top priority. Many directors already realize the need for short- and long-range planning of their bank's activities. Of course, there are quantitative goals to set for the bank—deposit growth, loan expansion, income, expenses, and net earnings. But just as important is strategic planning—planning the role the bank will assume in the future. Does the bank have an exceptional department that should be expanded to capture a larger segment of the market? Or does the bank operate better as a generalist, meeting all the banking needs of the community? Concentrating on the bank's strong points is one way of assuring growth.

Another important aspect of planning is keeping a forward eye on the industry. Many a potential commercial bank market has been lost by lack of foresight. Directors should keep a broad view of banking. Moreover, they should be open to innovation and ever watchful of how the bank might expand its services and maximize its profits.

Whatever the bank's long-range plans, make sure they are realistic but not too "comfortable." Goals should not be set simply to make directors and management look good for having reached them. Make periodic checks to be sure that bank policies are supporting goals, and be prepared to modify goals if they prove to be too lax, on the one hand, or too rigorous, on the other.

NOTES FOR PART I

1. 12 U.S.C. §461
2. 12 U.S.C. §222
3. 12 U.S.C. §1814
4. 12 U.S.C. 1844(b)
5. 12 U.S.C. 1844
6. 12 U.S.C. 1843(a)
7. David H. Friedman, *Essentials of Banking* (Wash., D.C.: American Bankers Association, 1982), p. 41.
8. 12 U.S.C. 1842(a)
9. William H. Kennedy, Jr., "The Future Direction of the Financial Services Industry" (Speech before the Committee on Banking, Housing and Urban Affairs, U.S. Senate, May 3, 1983), p. 8.
10. Kennedy, pg. 8.
11. Arthur Young & Co., *Assessment of Business Expansion Opportunities for Banking* (Wash., D.C.: American Bankers Association, 1983), pp. 28–29.
12. 12 U.S.C. §922(c)
13. 12 U.S.C. §§24 (seventh) and 335
14. 12 U.S.C. §371(a)(3)
15. 12 U.S.C. §84
16. 12 U.S.C. §481
17. 12 U.S.C. §461
18. 12 U.S.C. §1817
19. 12 U.S.C. §1822(b)
20. 12 U.S.C. §1823(c)
21. 12 U.S.C. §1823(e)
22. 12 U.S.C. §36
23. 12 U.S.C. §1818, for example
24. *Federal Reserve Bulletin* (June 1980), pp. 444–453.
25. 12 U.S.C. 3503
26. Kennedy, pg. 21 and Appendix B: "Bibliography of Usury Ceiling Studies" (22 studies cited from 1967–1981).
27. Kennedy, pp. 27–28.
28. Kennedy, pp. 29–30 (citing study by Peter Merril Associates for the American Bankers Association, January 1981).
29. S. 2134, S. 2181 and H.R. 3537 were introduced in 1983.

PART II:

The Board and Its Functions

In Part I, we examined the business of banking and stressed the great impact of change in the financial services industry. It is the board's responsibility to see that the bank remains sound and competitive in the midst of this change. As policymakers, bank directors must keep abreast of new developments and recognize their implications for both the short- and long-range operations of the bank. As governors of the bank's affairs, directors not only must be well informed, they must also be actively involved in guiding management, controlling operations, and evaluating bank performance.

Part II examines the nature of the board and explains the board's major functions and responsibilities.

7

The Board of Directors

Who are the bank's board of directors, what are their responsibilities and accountabilities, and how do they fulfill them? This chapter answers these questions by discussing the composition of the board; the selection, qualifications, and duties of directors; conditions of board service; and the directors' relationship with stockholders, management, and the community.

BOARD COMPOSITION

The board of directors is composed of top officers from within the bank (commonly known as *inside directors*) and business people from other professions (*outside directors*). There is no optimum ratio of inside to outside directors, but it is generally agreed that there should be more outside directors than inside directors. The best ratio is one that assures a balance of representation between the interests of the stockholders and the management of the bank. Neither inside nor outside directors should dominate or impose their judgments on the board. Freedom of expression, recognition of individual expertise, and mutual respect are essential for board effectiveness.

State laws vary regarding the size and composition of a bank's board, but for national banks and state banks that are Federal Reserve members, there must be between 5 and 25 directors,[1] one of whom is the bank president or CEO.[2] Bank boards are generally larger than corporate boards for several reasons: to bring a wide range of professional experience to bear on bank decision-making; to represent adequately the needs of the community served by the bank; and to secure important business accounts for the bank.

DIRECTOR SELECTION

Once a year, the bank holds a stockholders' meeting, which, under normal circumstances, is the only meeting open to nonboard members. A major function of the stockholders' meeting is the election of directors for the next year's term. A director's term is one year, but reelection is permitted indefinitely.

The bank stockholders are responsible for selecting board members who will most likely promote the success and economic growth of the bank and who will make effective decisions about whether management is doing its job. The board, together with bank management, usually recommends candidates to the stockholders for consideration, although stockholders also may suggest candidates. Some banks have nominating committees to identify prospective candidates and evaluate their qualifications and eligibility, and stockholders are encouraged to recommend candidates to the committee for nomination. It is the board's responsibility to insure continued sound stewardship of the bank by providing stockholders with the best qualified candidates for consideration.

QUALIFICATIONS

The stockholders and the board look for various qualities in an outside or nonbank director. Some qualifications, such as ownership of bank stock and residency requirements, are set by law. Clearly, the director candidate also must be qualified in terms of education, professional experience, business contacts, and special skills. Other less tangible but equally important qualifications include ethics, maturity, reputation, compatibility with other board members, diplomacy, and independent judgment.

Most banks have a minimum stock requirement for directors, and national bank directors *must* own capital stock (commonly referred to as "qualifying shares") in the bank. For directors of banks with capital stock of $25,000 or more, the total par value cannot be less than $1,000.[3] State-chartered banks also require a minimum investment, but the amounts vary. Directors of national banks that are owned by a bank holding company can own their qualifying shares in the stock of the holding company.

Major stockholders have a vested interest in the performance of the bank, and, similarly, a director whose investment is heavily at stake will usually be involved, conscientious, and hard-working. At times, however, these major stockholders may attempt to influence and dominate the board; this should be avoided in the best interests of the bank and the other stockholders.

Aside from ownership of bank stock, the law requires a national bank director to be a United States citizen. At least two-thirds of the directors must reside in the state where the bank is located, or within 100 miles of the bank for at least a year before election.[4] The law also prohibits any individual with a conflict of interest from serving as a director. Age requirements for directors are set in the bank's bylaws.

Proven good judgment and business sense are important qualifications for directors. The talents and expertise of individual board members should complement one another; therefore, the business skills of a prospective director should be related to a specific need of the board.

An ability to bring in business is another important qualification. The board may select a director for his or her extensive business contacts, with the expectation that some of this business will be brought to the bank. Care must be taken, though, to avoid conflicts of interest. The board should not put pressure on a director to bring in deposits of a corporation that may be better served by another institution. However, the board and the stockholders have a right to assume that a director will act in good faith to bring in business that will help the bank and that the bank can serve adequately.

The board member is in an excellent position to market bank services and should be intimately familiar with all the services the bank can offer in order to recommend them to prospective customers. This does not have to amount to an active "hard sell." However, when the opportunity to promote bank services presents itself, it should be seized.

A director should not make unilateral commitments for the bank. The board should discuss specific procedures for referring business to the bank so that misunderstandings or misrepresentations do not occur.

Prestige and community representation are additional qualities that the board may look for in a director. A bank's image is often enhanced by having prominent and respected citizens on its board. A positive image can help increase bank business. The board also may be interested in filling positions with representatives of the community, such as members of minority and special-interest groups or community business leaders.

DUTIES OF DIRECTORS

The specific duties of the board of directors vary with the size and type of bank, but all bank boards have the same major responsibilities. The members of the board represent the interests of the stockholders and are legally responsible for the sound management of the bank. It is the board's responsibility to see that management decisions are prudent, that the bank operates in compliance with government laws and regulations, and that bank performance shows profitability and growth. The board is accountable for bank results, and in some cases, personally liable for bank losses.

The board's duties can be grouped into four basic functions: selecting bank management, setting bank policies, controlling bank practices, and analyzing bank performance. The nature of these functions and the specific duties that may be associated with each function are examined in more detail in Chapter 8.

Generally speaking, board members cannot be expected to be involved with every aspect of bank operations. As a bank's business increases, the required research and decision-making become too massive for total participation by each director. For this reason many boards have opted for the committee system. Committees, which can be formed at the request of the stockholders or by a resolution of the board, are charged with the responsibility for researching a particular area of concern and making recommendations. In a report to the board, a committee presents salient documents, facts, and the recommended decision for discussion and approval. Many committees, such as the audit committee, may be permanent, while others may be interim. The committee system does not relieve individual directors of their general responsibility for supervision, but committees are a valuable concept in board activity.

Some bank boards provide directors with position descriptions that plainly state what activity and commitment the board expects of each member. The director's position description can be a useful tool for the board in interviewing prospective board members. The position description in Exhibit 3 indicates the scope and tone of such documents.

Exhibit 3
Bank Director's Sample
Position Description

Nature and Scope

As representatives of the stockholders, the board of directors exercises powers as conferred through the bank's Articles of Association and Bylaws. Members of the board of directors participate jointly in the overall supervision of the bank's affairs. Responsibilities of the board include, but are not limited to—

1. The continuity of the bank as a sound institution with adequate capital, skilled management, and well-defined policies.

2. The compliance with the laws and regulations imposed by governmental agencies.

3. The protection of stockholders, depositors, loan customers, and creditors, through internal control, independent audits, and insurance coverage.

4. The performance of duties with diligence and prudence.

Exhibit 3 continued

Functional Duties

To fulfill the responsibilities to the stockholders, depositors, and the community, the board of directors discharges its duties as a legislative body and as a plural executive team. The major functional duties of the bank director are:

1. To attend scheduled board of directors' meetings.
2. To select and appoint a competent chief executive officer.
3. To provide leadership in planning the overall affairs of the bank.
4. To determine with other members of the management group the short- and long-range goals of the bank.
5. To review, approve, and periodically evaluate the operating policies of the bank in such areas as dividend policy, lending policy, investment policy, security policy, personnel policy, conflict of interest and disclosure policies, and trust department policy.
6. To recognize problems or issues beyond the scope of the management of the bank.
7. To take remedial or corrective action when dealing with problems.
8. To safeguard the financial condition of the bank.
9. To approve operating and capital budgets.
10. To work continuously to advance the interests of the bank.

Bank Performance Responsibilities

Beyond the responsibilities to warrant that the bank is a sound institution and has skilled management, the bank director must make certain that the bank continues as a competitive business with satisfactory performance ratios and a competitive marketing strategy, and that it meets the needs and serves the legitimate interests of its market area. In particular a bank director should—

1. Review and critically examine such common ratios and performance measurements as: return on equity; return on assets; loans-to-deposits ratio; loans-to-capital ratio; bank liquidity; employee cost per dollar of deposit; quick-asset ratio; debt-to-net-worth ratio; cost of funds.
2. Review and evaluate the marketing strategy and marketing plan and monitor the bank's ability to achieve goals.

Other Responsibilities

In addition to the regular duties, the bank director must be alert to changes in the industry, the need for corporate reorganization, the possibilities of acquisition or merger, and a multitude of other duties, such as the following:

1. Serve on bank committees.
2. Make recommendations to the stockholders concerning the size of the board and new members.
3. Establish a retirement age for directors.
4. Make recommendations for amendments to the Articles of Association or Bylaws.
5. Propose the appointment of outside auditors and review audit reports.
6. Recommend the removal of board members for cause.

CONDITIONS OF SERVICE

Bank directors assume a number of legal responsibilities as a condition of service. In addition to these legal concerns, directors must be aware of bank standards for compensation and retirement.

Legal Concerns

Bank directors, like directors of other corporations, bear the traditional corporate responsibilities of ensuring that the bank is operated in a sound and profitable manner that leads to future growth. Unlike most other businesses, banking is governed by numerous laws and statutes, and bank directors have legal responsibilities that are specific to banking. Thus, bank directors must be concerned with responsibilities of criminal law, common law, and statutory law at both the state and federal levels.

National bank directors are required to take a personal oath that they will administer the affairs of the bank with honesty and diligence, and that they will not knowingly violate or permit the violation of banking laws.[5] Most state banks require similar oaths. Directors can be held personally liable for damages resulting from a violation of banking statutes. Willfull intent is a key aspect of personal liability in the violation of banking statutes, but ignorance of such statutes is not a defense against personal liability—the director is presumed to know the law.

In addition to being fully aware of the bank's legal requirements and ensuring bank compliance with such requirements, directors are legally responsible for carrying out their duties in a conscientious manner. Standards for director performance generally are broadly defined: the director is expected to behave as a prudent and reasonable person, exercising ordinary care and diligence and acting in good faith. These standards, by their nature, show that the director is not legally accountable for every action of the bank's officers or for every aspect of the bank's daily operations, but the director *is* legally responsible for showing common sense, thoroughness, and loyalty in supervising the affairs of the bank. This includes careful selection of the bank's chief executive officer and evaluation of other officers; diligent supervision of bank management and bank operations; attentiveness to the findings and suggestions of bank auditors and examiners; and avoidance of conflicts of interest or self-interest in the director's own business affairs.

Part III of this book explores the nature and scope of the director's legal responsibilities in the areas of statutory law, criminal law, common law, securities law, and antitrust law; explains the enforcement actions, procedures, and penalties of regulatory agencies; and discusses director insurance and indemnification.

Compensation

Director compensation varies in amount and type, depending on bank size and degree of director involvement. Some boards are paid an annual salary; others are paid on a per-meeting basis. Some banks combine an annual retainer with per-meeting payments to recognize director involvement. Director compensation should be competitive with that of other boards of directors of similar size banks in the area.

Retirement and Separation

Retirement is a sensitive issue for many directors. An individual who loses his or her effectiveness as a director due to age or infirmity owes it to the board and the bank to step down, but this does not always happen. A written retirement policy is an obvious answer to the problem. Although the need is evident, not enough bank boards have formal retirement policies because of the difficulty of matching chronological age with loss of effectiveness and because of the sensitivity of senior directors to the issue of retirement.

There are at least two paths the board can take to standardize the issue of retirement. A "grandfather" clause can exempt current board members from the new policy. A second option is to create a "director emeritus" position so that retired directors can continue to provide valuable input to the board. A director emeritus would have no legal vote on the board, but would also be free from most forms of legal liability. A fair retirement policy eliminates the discomfort of having to deal with the issue each time it occurs.

A director is obligated to offer full commitment to the bank and maintain business integrity. If, before retirement age, a director feels that he or she can no longer contribute the time and attention needed to effectively fulfill his or her duties, the director has an obligation to step down. Similarly, in a conflict of interest situation, the director must choose between the bank and another business interest.

ACCOUNTABILITY OF DIRECTORS

The board is accountable—or called upon to give an explanation for action—to the stockholders, the depositors, the public, and various regulatory agencies. Frequently, the interests of these groups overlap; often, however, their desires conflict, and they may not all be pleased by the same action.

An example of conflicting desires might involve excess liquidity. Although excess liquidity may be beneficial to depositors, it could restrict lending, thus hurting borrowers; excess liquidity also might lower earnings, which would be of concern to the stockholders. A too liberal lending policy might also cause problems: it might be beneficial to borrowers, but could lead to high-risk, marginal loans, and problems of capital adequacy—problems that would concern the stockholders.

Simply put, board members need to balance the bank's affairs so that they comply with legal requirements and give maximum satisfaction to those to whom the board is accountable.

The Stockholders

As their elected representatives, directors must be accountable to the stockholders, who are primarily interested in the return on their investment. Stockholders assume the majority of risk by investing in the bank, and profits are the incentive. It is also in the best interests of the stockholders to combine profitability with safety. Toward this end, the directors are accountable for the long-range growth and stability of the bank.

A well-planned budget should be an important part of the bank's overall profit planning. Directors can use the budget to compare projected status with actual status, thereby keeping a constant watch on bank operations. Specific methods of analyzing bank performance are discussed in Chapter 8.

The Depositors

The relationship between the bank and the depositor is contractual, and responsibilities are imposed on both parties. Of primary importance to the depositor is the safety of funds.

The safety of bank capital has been greatly increased by federal control. If a bank has poor earnings, loose internal control, or highly speculative assets, regulatory examiners will usually intercede before capital adequacy is impaired. The examiners, who must be assured of a bank's solvency and soundness, will look at the following components for this assurance:

- quality of management;

- liquidity of assets;

- history and retention of earnings;

- occupancy expenses;

- potential volatility of deposit structure;

- operating procedures; and

- capacity to meet present and projected financial needs.

Directors are also accountable to depositors in maintaining competitive services and interest rates. Banks must hold their share of the total market in a keenly competitive environment.

Finally, depositors are interested in the convenience of the bank and its services. Easily reached premises, automation, and EFT services are examples of bank efforts to meet customers' needs for convenient services.

The Public and Community Responsibility

Sensitivity of banks to their social responsibilities is becoming greater every year. Bank management and directors, as business and professional people, are expected to be active in community affairs and organizations. But public accountability and responsibility to the community mean more than this.

Regulatory agencies are becoming increasingly active in ensuring that banks meet the needs of the communities they serve. This is because the boundaries of "community" have blurred with expanding bank operations and an increase in bank branching and banking across state lines. Because of these developments, community needs are not as apparent or as immediate as they once were, and standards for public accountability and community service are now being proscribed rather than left to the judgment of directors. Directors and management must work together to ensure that the bank complies with legal standards regarding employment and employee advancement, service to consumers and consumer protection, and meeting the credit needs of all members of the community.

Commercial banks and other depository institutions are experiencing increased attention from enforcement authorities in the area of equal employment opportunity. All banks must have an affirmative action program and must insure that they provide for employment, training, and advancement.[6] Failure to do so could result in a costly lawsuit.

The growing number and variety of bank products available to consumers, the development of new banking technologies such as electronic funds transfer, and mounting public concern for protection and privacy, have given rise to many new consumer protection requirements in recent years. Directors must work with bank management, legal counsel, and state and federal regulators to stay informed of new requirements in these areas.

A specific law that directors must be concerned about is the Community Reinvestment Act of 1977,[7] which prohibits discrimination in commercial, business, residential, and agricultural credit. The act requires an examination of the bank's performance in meeting the credit needs of the entire community, consistent with the safe and sound operations of those banks. Further, approval for expanded bank operations depends on the applicant's record in meeting the credit needs of the entire community.[8] The bank's role in supporting the community might be established through community development and urban renewal projects. Equally important is the availability of loans for minority businesses and housing. The bank's planning for the future should be coordinated with the community's plans in an effort to meet mutual goals.

The director's legal responsibilities and liabilities in these and other areas are discussed further in Part III of this book.

8

The Functions of the Board

The board has both functional and legal responsibilities. Although they are treated separately here for purposes of discussion, these responsibilities are interdependent. (The board's legal responsibilities are discussed in Part III of this book.) Here we will examine the board's functional responsibilities—selecting bank management, setting bank policies, controlling bank practices, and analyzing bank performance.

SELECTING BANK MANAGEMENT

The primary function of the board of directors is selecting and maintaining top-quality senior management. Obvious qualities to look for in a potential chief executive officer are leadership, analytical ability, a realistic outlook, and a strong, well-documented record of accomplishment in banking. The potential CEO's qualifications should match the bank's objectives. For example, if the board has decided on a particular set of objectives for the bank over the next five years, a CEO should be selected who agrees with these goals and is capable of leading the bank toward their achievement.

Board members must decide the level of personal involvement needed in the selection of bank officers and other employees. Generally, senior management should assume primary responsibility for the selection of employees, as long as board policies are followed and board approval is sought on final decisions.

Hiring and keeping good management do not end with an interview and a placement. The board must make sure that salaries and benefits are competitive in the industry, or the top people will look elsewhere for positions. The board should also plan for management succession by staffing officer-trainee positions or the equivalents with a view to such employees' future competence as officers. Promising employees should be recognized and prepared for movement into top management positions.

Whomever the board chooses for the bank's management, an understanding of management's relationship to the board and management's responsibilities should be clear from the beginning. Directors are there to oversee and direct. Management is there to execute the directives. A board may let its management suggest board policies, but adoption is the ultimate responsibility of the board.

SETTING BANK POLICIES

The formulation of bank policy is a key process in a bank's long-range planning. Today, because of rapid changes in technology, competition, and regulation, greater numbers of banks are recognizing the need for long-range planning. Such continuous change calls for planning, not only for the immediate future but for many years ahead, if the bank is to remain viable in the marketplace and maintain its profitability.

Planning requires the full commitment of the board, the CEO, and the bank's officers. To succeed, a plan must have the endorsement of senior management, the active participation of all bank officers, and an adequate commitment of time for implementation. Planning is grounded in the bank's mission statement, which broadly defines the bank's basic purpose or business and the scope or limits of the bank's operations.

Planning involves several steps. First, it must be built on a foundation of information that is obtained by analyzing the bank's present condition and its future possibilities. Internal analysis examines the bank's past record of performance and identifies the bank's major strengths and weaknesses; external analysis examines the possible impact on the bank (either positive or negative) of economic, competitive, legal, technological, and social factors. Assumptions are made, based on these analyses, and are clarified and formalized as objectives of bank policy. These objectives then must be broken down into specific steps or strategies for implementation.

An objective is a formal statement of intent or goal that usually dictates a specific course of action. An objective differs from a strategy because it expresses a philosophy or is a statement of intent. A strategy, on the other hand, is an actual course of action. For example, an objective may require that the bank have 10 percent of its capital invested in long-term maturities. The strategy statement would include specific information about which securities, the maturity dates, and the dollar amounts.

Bank directors bear the final responsibility for setting bank objectives, although the degree of board involvement in policy development varies from bank to bank; the board may participate actively in writing policy, or it may review and approve policy once it is written. The development of strategies to implement policy objectives is chiefly the responsibility of bank management.

Several points should be kept in mind with regard to setting bank policy:

- A policy is a statement of intent or goal—not a specific course of action.
- Policies state the bank's objectives over a long period of time; strategies state how objectives will be implemented given current and expected conditions.
- Policies should be written and should become part of the bank files.
- Policies should include provisions for their review and updating at regular intervals.

Once the bank's policies have been established, the board must constantly monitor their implementation. Monitoring a policy means making a periodic assessment of the bank's current status relative to the policy. To that end, procedures for monitoring should be established, including detailed reviews of the examiners' reports and management reports. Any deviation from a policy should be looked into and corrected.

For purposes of example, guidelines on policy development are highlighted in the following sections for some major policy areas—lending, investments, trusts, personnel, and security. Other policy areas could include asset/liability management, internal controls and audits, and marketing, among others. Regulatory requirements also call for additional policies: affirmative action plans, consumer protection, and community reinvestment are some examples.

Lending Policy

The lending policy is among the most important policies a bank can have. If a bank has no lending policy or a weak one, it risks excessive extensions of credit, more volume than can be handled adequately by the staff, and/or a reduction in bank liquidity. It is as important for the board to supervise the nature and extent of loans as it is for the bank to make them. Following are some items not to be overlooked in developing a loan policy:

- *Relating loan policy to the bank's objectives.* First, the bank must identify its primary customers in the community and define its degree of service in terms of commercial, real estate, and consumer loans. The board then must decide parameters within which loans will be made by defining acceptable or undesirable risks, establishing procedures for asset/liability management, and assessing the availability of funds. Setting the percentage of funds available for commercial loans, consumer loans, and mortgage loans is a crucial part of the loan policy. It determines the bank's ability to adapt to the economy, to get maximum income from interest, and to attract deposits from the community.

- *Loan responsibility and authority.* The second step in formulating the lending policy is to determine which officers are responsible for loan approval and to establish lending limits. It is obviously good practice to give higher lending authority (dollar limit on loans made without direct board approval) to officers in responsible positions. And even higher lending authority can be given to combinations of officers when the loan request exceeds an individual officer's authority. Ultimate responsibility for loan approval beyond a specified dollar limit rests with the board. The limit, of course, varies with the size of the bank.

- *Geographic limits for generating loans.* Establishing a bank's trade area is important in limiting the risk factor and also in developing community relations. If the bank over-extends its geographic boundaries, it cannot adequately serve the market in its own community. Many bankers admit that their worst losses occurred when they loaned outside their normal market.

- *Maximum maturity periods for different types of loans.* A primary function of the board is to establish maximum term and schedule policies for loan repayment. This will vary depending on the type of loan (consumer, real estate, commercial, agricultural), and whether the loans are secured or unsecured.

- *Minimum interest rates.* The interest rate policy depends on several factors. Although minimum rates must be established for different types of loans, standards should be set for the use of above-minimum interest rates. Rate differentials should be determined in relation to such factors as risk, repayment schedules, account relationships, and amount of bank service involved.

- *Appraisal policies and maximum percentage of appraised value to be loaned.* In making mortgage loans, the bank's policy should reflect standard, nondiscriminatory procedures for appraising the value of the property. The percentage downpayment required or, conversely, the maximum percentage of the appraised value to be loaned, should be stated in the policy. Directors should continually evaluate the objectivity of persons making appraisals for the bank.

- *Credit information.* The lending policy should set forth the types of credit information required for different types of loans. A first-rate credit practice is the key to a successful loan policy, and most banks have one set of credit standards for business loans and another for consumer loans. Furthermore, many banks require more detailed information from new customers of the bank than from regular customers. When deciding creditworthiness, the loan policy should consider financial statements, historical records, and collateral. Written reasons for deviations from the credit policy should be available or be reported to the board for approval, and a note of the deviation should be kept with the loan file.

- *Governmental restrictions.* Maximum limits on loans are usually regulated by state or federal agencies. The creativity with which the loan policy is administered within these restrictions is up to the board and management. The government also regulates the form and content of loan documents. Regulation Z (truth in lending), the Real Estate Settlement Procedures Act, and Regulation B (equal credit opportunity) are among those laws and regulations requiring board attention.

Investment Policy

A good investment policy, like a loan policy, is vital to bank profitability. A weak investment policy makes the bank susceptible to income losses from failure to invest excess funds or from making investments that have to be liquidated prematurely at a loss.

Federal government and municipal securities form the greater part of bank investment portfolios. To formulate the overall goals of the investment policy, the board should understand the purpose and nature of bank reserves and the money market. A knowledge of the money market provides a sensitivity to fluctuations in the rates of securities.

Smaller banks rely somewhat on correspondent banks for investment tactics because they often do not have the staff necessary to research and formulate an investment policy. However, directors are cautioned that responsibility for investment policy is theirs alone. Blind reliance on a correspondent will not necessarily avoid liability if the bank suffers a loss.

Following are a few points to consider in developing an investment policy:

- *Determine the size of the investment portfolio.* The size of the bank's investment portfolio should, at the very minimum, cover its liquidity needs. Liquidity needs can be estimated by relating loan and deposit histories to economic trends. The amount and types of investments should first cover the projected liquidity needs of the bank, thereby supporting the loan policy. Other investments may be considered after liquidity is assured.

- *Stagger maturity dates for invested cash.* The maturity dates of securities must be constantly appraised. Ideally, if interest rates are rising, the portfolio should consist of short-term maturities. Upon maturity, higher-yielding securities could be repurchased. Conversely, if the interest rates are falling, the investment portfolio would benefit from long-term maturities. Even though economic forecasting is not precise enough to advise the bank of the ideal situation, it is useful as a policy tool. Generally, the maturity dates of the bank's investments should coincide with the bank's perceived needs for liquidity.

- *Rationally weigh profitability and risk factors.* There is risk, in terms of income loss, in the quality of certain state or local securities and corporate bonds. This risk involves the deterioration of these bonds and securities over time, and the potential loss of funds for the bank. In some cases, even if a long-term maturity seems to be more profitable, the risk factor may dictate the purchase of short-term maturities. In all decisions regarding the purchase of long- or short-term securities, the expected profit should be considered in relation to the nature of the security and the risk involved.

- *Include qualitative and quantitative restraints imposed by regulatory agencies.* Regulatory agencies stipulate that bank investments not be speculative in nature. Both national banks and federally regulated state banks are prohibited from including equity issues in their investment portfolios. There are also limitations on the amount of certain types of securities a bank may hold in relation to its capital and surplus accounts.

- *Relate tax status to the number of tax-exempt bonds.* The board should be familiar with the bank's tax bracket and its yearly taxable income. Tax-exempt bonds can be used to improve the tax position of the bank.

An astute investment policy can mean substantial earnings for the bank. The policy should be monitored by a board-appointed investment officer and should be reappraised from time to time in relation to loan demand and deposit growth.

Trust Policy

Approximately 4,000 of the nation's banks offer specialized trust services, which may range from settling an estate to acting as an agent for an employee benefit account.

Within the bank, the trust department operates separately from other bank activities, with its assets separate and distinct. Because of its unique position in the bank's organizational structure and the nature of the trust department's fiduciary responsibility, a clear trust policy is essential.

Directors of banks with trust departments are directly responsible for establishing, communicating, and ensuring that the trust policy is implemented. A trust department policy should contain guidelines in the following areas:

- *The legal and ethical basis.* Trust departments operate under rules established by common law, state law, Regulation 9 (issued by the Comptroller of the Currency),[9] provisions of the Glass-Steagall Act of 1933, the Pension Reform Act of 1974,[10] and other laws. The requirements and procedures for complying with these various laws should be clearly spelled out in a bank's trust policy.

- *Management philosophy.* The board establishes the guidelines defining the departmental organization and delegation. Important matters here are the limits and constraints on personnel and the degree of freedom and accountability. Also, these guidelines must be compatible with the bank's overall philosophy.

- *Investment philosophy.* Of primary importance in trust policy are guidelines for investment. Trust investment policy differs from overall bank investment policy mainly in that the trust department invests the customers' money (not the bank's), and investments may be made in corporate stocks on behalf of customers (the bank itself cannot make such investments). In accord with the terms and goals of each trust, the trustee selects appropriate investment vehicles. In most states, the trustee follows the "prudent man rule," which states that the trustee should use "prudence, discretion, and intelligence . . . in considering the probable income, as well as the probable safety of the capital to be invested."

  The trust policy should specify acceptable fields of investment, noting low-risk and high-risk stocks, as well as securities considered to be sound investments.

- *Internal control and audit procedures.* Trust policy also deals with internal control and audit procedures. National banks are required to conduct trust department audits at least once a year, and the board should oversee strict audit procedures on trust department activities. Usually, the board designates a trust committee (composed of board members and management) or employs an outside CPA or firm to monitor trust procedures and controls. However, the legal responsibility for administering trust agreements remains with the entire board, and comprehensive audit procedures are the best assurance against mismanagement of funds.

Personnel Policy

Employee relations—the entire spectrum of activities that affect people at work—is one basis for a bank's success: profitable services hinge on how well employees carry out their responsibilities. Good employee relations can also make important contributions to productivity and stability in the staff and can help reduce absenteeism and internal friction.

But good employee relations don't come about by chance. They are usually the result of formal personnel policies, established practices to put such policies into effect, and controls or audits designed to monitor them to make sure they actually work.

The personnel policies and their implementation are also subject to numerous and complex laws and regulations with which banks must comply. These cover hiring, promotion, transfer, and training procedures, as well as wages, hours, and other conditions of employment.

- *Complying with the Equal Employment Opportunity Commission Guidelines.* The Equal Employment Opportunity Commission (EEOC) was established to guarantee the rights of all people to fair employment opportunity, regardless of race, color, religion, sex, or national origin.[11]

  The EEOC's guidelines declare that no hiring, promotion, transfer, or training procedure may be used in personnel selection unless it can be shown that the procedure does not discriminate against any minority and is a good indicator of future job performance.[12] Banks, by virtue of their visibility and responsibility to their communities, should be forerunners in compliance with these guidelines. For banks, the designated compliance agency is the Department of Labor.

  Every bank in the United States having deposits of federal funds and every bank that is an issuing and paying agent of savings bonds and notes is required by Executive Order 11246, as amended, to develop and implement an affirmative action program on an annual basis. Exempted, however, from requirements to have a *written* plan are employers with less than 50 employees. Although most community banks are in the exempt category, it is important, nevertheless, that any discriminatory practice be eliminated to ensure compliance with the law and to avoid employee complaints or lawsuits.

  A policy statement on equal employment opportunity and affirmative action must convey the bank's commitment to the concept and practice of equal employment and affirmative action and should serve as a guide to bank management responsible for carrying out the policy. Such a policy is a key standard by which the bank's actions and attitude in the equal opportunity area are measured by employees and the community.

Many banks already have affirmative action programs through which they are staffing high-level positions with competent women and minorities. As employees become more aware of their rights, banks, along with any other employers, become more vulnerable to legal accusations of unfair employment practices. Any bank, from the largest to the smallest, is best protected from this by initiating, documenting, and carrying out an affirmative action program in compliance with the EEOC. The EEOC guidelines are still being formulated and are subject to change, so the board should consult the bank's legal counsel and pertinent literature in this area.

- *Establishing an equitable salary administration and benefits program.* No matter what size the bank is, it is important for it to have a clearly defined salary administration program. The objectives of such a program should be:

  —to attract, retain, and motivate appropriately qualified individuals at all levels of the bank;
  —to pay salaries that relate to the value of each position in the bank;
  —to compensate employees in relation to their performance;
  —to provide clear guidelines and procedures for salary administration; and
  —to provide a means for budgeting and controlling salary expense.

The concept of matching competing salaries applies from the lowest-paid bank positions to the highest. Being competitive in salaries with other financial institutions and with comparable jobs in the community is one way of getting and keeping good employees with the necessary ability and commitment.

In connection with salary administration, under federal wage and hour laws and related legislation, employers are required to meet specified standards with respect to minimum wages, hours, and other conditions of employment.[13]

Directors should be aware of the provisions of these statutes and the accompanying regulations and keep abreast of
new developments, so they can assure the bank's compliance.

Besides salaries, however, a sound compensation and
personnel program includes the following benefits:

Opportunity for mobility—Employees appreciate the
opportunity for movement within the bank, whether
lateral or vertical. Likewise, promotions encourage and
reward good workers. Obviously, favoritism should not
be a reason for promotion since it can only cause resent-
ment and dissatisfaction. Senior officers are not exempt
from scrutiny, and the board should give them regular
performance evaluations and recognition for achievement.

Opportunity for employee development—Another
way to assure mobility and keep employees up-to-date
on banking issues and innovations is to provide for their
continuing education. Programs sponsored by the American Bankers Association, the American Institute of
Banking, the Bank Administration Institute, the Bank
Marketing Association, state bankers associations, and
others cover a wide range of banker education programs.

The board should determine the bank's policy on education assistance. Some alternatives are complete or par-
tial tuition reimbursement (already standard in many
banks), time off for classes, and time for in-bank seminars.

Attendance at bankers' meetings and conferences—
An excellent forum for hearing the latest about banking
is the banking-related meetings or conventions. It is
important to send representatives to meetings relevant to
the bank, for the new ideas to be gleaned, for good business contracts, and for employee morale. Many such
opportunities are also available for bank directors.

Employees as customers—One issue that each bank
must decide is whether or not it wants its own employees' business. Some banks require their staffs to do their
banking at other institutions in order to minimize the
temptation of tampering with the books. Other banks
find equal justification for requiring employees'
accounts to be carried in their bank.

Fringe benefits—A good fringe benefit package acts to attract new employees and to retain current ones. Benefits such as health plans, holidays, and employee stock ownership are ways of showing employees that the bank cares about their well-being. Pension plans are a major fringe benefit, although recent regulation on pension plans has made it very difficult for small banks to maintain them. For example, the Employment Retirement Income Security Act of 1974 places employers in the onerous position of trustee of employee pension funds.[14]

Since small banks may find pension payments and associated paperwork difficult and expensive, their directors may want to consider alternatives. Such alternatives include profit-sharing plans, in which contributions are made on a percentage basis rather than in a fixed amount, and Individual Retirement Accounts (IRAs), which are opened by individual employees but may be facilitated by the bank.

A good set of fringe benefits can increase morale and improve the tax status of employees. Remember, however, that bonuses and profit-sharing are never a substitute for adequate salaries. The board should not hestitate to call in benefits consultants to assist in the formulation and implementation of a comprehensive employee benefits program.

- *Establishing a policy on labor relations.* The labor relations area is complex because it involves the nature of unions themselves—their goals and methods. It involves law. And it involves employees—how they feel about their jobs, bank policies, and their supervisors. The field of labor relations is a specialty that a bank's board should not take lightly or without seeking expert guidance, for a bank must ensure that it is acting within the law and must know what it can and cannot do in the event of a union drive in the bank.

Although unions have made relatively few inroads into the banking industry, the evidence is clear that, because of the vast numbers of bank personnel as potential members, unions are intensifying their efforts to organize banks.

Sound employee relations policies and practices and their effective administration are the essential ingredients in employee satisfaction, which is the major force in resisting unionization of employees.

- *Hiring a personnel/benefits manager.* A highly qualified, full-time personnel/benefits manager should be an integral part of the bank's management team. This person can potentially save the bank large amounts of money, time, and adverse publicity by properly administering the bank's personnel and benefits function.

Security Policy

The Bank Protection Act of 1968[15] made into law what had been a growing practice in banks: a security officer must be appointed who reports directly to the board of directors on matters of security programs and devices.

For the protection of personnel, customers, assets, and equipment, it is important that the board set clearly defined security guidelines. The bank's security policy should be researched and written under the guidance of the security officer, and then approved by the board. Its emphasis should be on safety first, for both employees and customers.

Once the overall policy is decided upon, the board should oversee the establishment of a plan or blueprint to achieve the security goals. The board should check with the local police force about adequate physical protection. Many advances have been made in photo detection and alarm systems, but the bank, to be adequately protected, does not have to look like a fortress. Again, the board-appointed security officer should be in charge of implementing the plan through training of personnel, installation of equipment, and establishment of security procedures.

The main ingredient of a security system is a well-prepared and educated staff, for the best alarm system money can buy will be useless if bank personnel do not know how or when to activate it. The bank's security officer should hold seminars and conduct drills with the staff. Literature is available to guide banks in setting up security procedures.

CONTROLLING BANK PRACTICES

Bank operations and practices must be monitored regularly and frequently by means of both internal controls/ audits and examinations by regulatory agencies. Examinations conducted by or for the regulatory agencies differ from internal controls and audits conducted by or for the bank. The primary responsibility for assuring proper audits and for establishing internal controls rests with the board of directors. Directors are also responsible for taking corrective action to bring the bank in compliance with regulations, should external examinations warrant.

Internal Controls and Audits

Directors are responsible for monitoring bank practices by establishing a system of internal controls and then seeing that control procedures are followed by means of audits. Internal controls involve every conceivable means of protecting the bank from losses, ranging from broad management policies to simple, routine procedures. Control procedures should seek to minimize the temptation for dishonesty. Such precautionary measures as separating the teller and bookkeeper functions, enforcing mandatory vacations, requiring dual signatures on expense checks and overdrafts, and rotating employees can ward off embezzlement or fraud.

Internal audits are used to identify and correct problems before they surface in examinations by regulatory agencies. To achieve this, audits seek to verify the accuracy of the bank's financial reports. This requires verification of five major account categories: assets, liabilities, income, expenses, and net worth.

An auditor appointed by the board takes responsibility for the audits. A formal program should be designed so that all departments and branches are audited periodically (at least once a year). To be effective, an audit should come as a complete surprise to the bank personnel involved, including top management. Therefore, the auditor may present an audit plan to the board, but specific dates should not be divulged. As an agent of the board, the auditor is in a good position to see that operating safeguards and controls are maintained. Any deviation should be reported.

It is evident from this discussion that independence is an important characteristic of the audit function. The scope of the auditor's activities and reporting responsibilities is often spelled out in the bylaws or in a special resolution of the board, and the auditor should report only to the board of directors.

Banks should seek assistance as needed in setting up an adequate internal control and audit system. One source is the bank regulatory agencies, which are willing to advise bank boards on internal controls and audit procedures.

External Examinations

Internal and external audits attempt to uncover embezzlement and fraud as well as to determine that adequate accounting practices are in place. External examinations are also concerned with the soundness, safety, and legal compliance of bank operations.

Bank examinations conducted by the regulatory agencies are not limited to analysis and appraisal of financial reports. The examiners also appraise quality and effectiveness of management, the loan and investment portfolios, the bank's capital adequacy, the equity position, and the bank's operating performance.

Appraisal is the distinguishing activity of bank examiners as opposed to internal auditors. Although the auditor's authority varies among banks, it is generally limited to verification and does not include appraisals. Examiners *rate* the quality of a loan, whereas auditors *verify* the obligation as genuine; examiners also check for compliance with applicable laws and regulations. The fact that the bank has recently undergone an examination in no way lessens the need for internal audits and controls. The examiners are interested in the bank's solvency and its compliance with regulations rather than with preventing defalcations. Such problems may be far advanced before the examiner's next visit.

As part of their appraisals, bank examiners look at the bank's financial records and departmental data, its policies and procedures (including internal control and audit procedures), its internal reports and operating materials (forms, worksheets, etc.), and sometimes minutes of board meetings. All audit findings and examination reports must be carefully reviewed by the board, and any deficiencies or exceptions corrected.

ANALYZING BANK PERFORMANCE

As already noted, profitability is essential to bank survival and growth. The bank's stockholders must receive an adequate return on their investments or they will make future investments elsewhere. Profitability is also a measure of the bank's effectiveness in serving the needs of the public, for if banks are not competitive, profitability cannot be maintained.

Analyzing the bank's performance in terms of both short-term budgeting and long-term growth is an extremely important function of the board. To meet its responsibilities and accountabilities to stockholders, depositors, the community, and regulatory agencies, the board must regularly examine the bank's effectiveness in managing its resources.

Measures of bank performance are comparative; a bank's performance is measured against its past record of performance and against the performance of other banks. Thus, the board has two indicators of bank performance: self-comparison and peer comparisons.

Self-Comparison

The board should regularly receive management reports on the bank's status. The frequency of reports and the amount of information contained may vary from bank to bank, but reports most helpful to the board are those that help identify and analyze meaningful trends or deviations from established goals. Comparisons of the bank's current monthly performance to the previous year, year-to-date, and the current year's profit plan are most helpful.

Table 3 shows a number of reports that may be presented to the board, describes them briefly, and suggests frequency of presentation. This information should be adapted to the bank's needs—some of the reports may not apply, or their content or frequency may require change. Also, if the board meets weekly, it may want to adjust this schedule. For example, certain reports may require weekly review, while others would more appropriately be considered on a monthly basis.

In using these reports to measure the bank's performance, the board should consider the following guidelines:

- *Liquidity*. The composition of deposits has an effect on the primary and secondary reserves. Demand deposits are normally more volatile and require more primary and secondary reserves than time deposits.

  The ratio of quick assets to deposits measures the bank's ability to cover all deposits. However, it is unlikely that all depositors will need their money at the same time.

  Seasonal movements in the community can be good indicators of a bank's liquidity needs. But unexpected loan demands or deposit withdrawals from large customers could adversely affect the bank. Bank management should be familiar with customers' business activities and anticipate their needs when planning liquidity requirements.

- *Loan to Deposit Ratio*. This ratio has some limitations, but it can be used as an inverse indicator of liquidity. A high ratio indicates the bank has invested a large portion of usable funds in loans. If the loanable position is out of line with the "average," it would be prudent to ascertain the reason for loan expansion and the types of borrowers served. A rising ratio may require more selective and cautious lending policies.

- *Return on Assets*. Return on assets shows the relationship between profits and assets, and tells how efficiently assets are used. The ratio of total assets (loans and investments) to available funds (deposits, capital funds less fixed assets, and borrowed money) indicates the total invested position of the bank. The return on assets is derived by dividing the income by the total assets. As noted earlier, return on assets is an important measure of bank performance because a bank's profitability may decline, even though its earnings are growing, if assets are not put to good use.

Table 3
Data for Self-Comparison

Report	Content	Presented
Comparative Balance Sheet	Asset and liability accounts compared with previous periods	monthly
Comparative Income and Expense Statement	Categories of income and expenses broken down to show current results of bank operations compared to the previous periods	monthly
Operating Ratios	Measures the results of bank operations in terms of ratios (such as earnings per share; return on stockholders' equity; capital to deposits; loans to deposits)	monthly or quarterly
Bank Liquidity	Form and maturity of assets related to anticipated demand for funds	monthly
Investments Report	Maturity of portfolio by category; market value, appreciation, and depreciation; securities bought and sold	monthly
Loans	New loans, renewals, large payouts, review of loans of a certain predetermined amount; problem loans	monthly
Past-Due Loans	Delinquent loans over a predetermined amount; comments and action being taken; delinquency percentage on loans, by type	monthly
Loans Recommended for Charge-Off	Borrower; amount; date and amount of loan; collateral; recovery possibility; lending officer	monthly
Auditor's Report	Progress and details of internal audit program, including exceptions	monthly
Profit Plan Forecast and Performance	Variances from plan and explanation of variances	quarterly
Cost of Funds	Funds borrowed and sold through the Fed or a correspondent bank	monthly
Department Reports	Trust department earnings, expenses, new business; branch operations; personnel activities	quarterly
Capital Accounts	Credits to undivided profits; dividends; other charges or expenses to capital accounts	quarterly
Reserve Accounts	Written-off assets and recoveries	quarterly
New Business	Significant new and closed accounts; business development activities of bank officers	quarterly
Marketing	Deposit growth, public relations; advertising; market penetration	semi-annually
Security Policy Review	Education and training programs conducted; security equipment; report on robberies	yearly
Planning	Annual budget; goals for coming year	yearly

- *Return on Equity.* Return on equity shows the relationship between profits and the stockholders' investment, and tells how efficiently equity capital is invested. This can be a good measure of the bank's performance compared to previous years. Earnings per share divided by the book value per share shows the rate of return. Also, if a bank's capital accounts only consist of common stock, surplus, undivided profits, and reserves, the net income can be divided by the total of the capital accounts to obtain the return on equity.

- *Deposit Mix.* Demand, time, and savings deposits are determining factors for the bank's reserve requirements, liquidity, allocation among earning assets of secondary reserves, and earning power. Increased movement in time and savings deposits has been attributed to the availability of higher yielding money market instruments. To be more competitive, banks have increased the interest they pay on accounts, but changes in the deposit mix or source of funds must be considered in relation to the use of funds.

- *Capital Adequacy.* This term relates the size of the bank's capital funds to the volume of deposits and assets. Capital funds are used to set lending and investment limits, investments in bank premises, and other qualitative and quantitative guides pertaining to bank operations.

  The ratio of capital funds to assets is an indicator of the bank's solvency or its ability to absorb possible losses in assets. For all practical purposes, a bank becomes insolvent if the common stock account is impaired by losses.

  There is no definitive answer to the question of how much capital is enough. However, several ratios can be used in analyzing capital adequacy: capital to loans, capital to risk assets, capital to total deposits, and capital to total assets.

- *Operating Efficiency.* The conventional test of operating efficiency is the ratio of total operating expenses to total operating income. Rates of returns on loans, interest cost on deposits, provision for loan losses to loans, and net loan losses to loans are other useful measures.

Peer Comparisons

In order to have a true picture of performance, comparisons must be made with the bank's peers as well as with the bank's own past record. Bank statements and operating performance should be compared with those of other similar banks. Ratios and performance indicators of other banks are easily obtained in reports from the regulatory agencies. Because the averages presented in these reports do not necessarily indicate good performance, they should be weighed in relation to your bank's objectives. Reports available from the regulatory agencies are listed in Table 4.

Table 4
Data for Peer Comparisons

Publication	Available From	Description
1. Functional Cost Analysis	Federal Reserve Board (annually)	Presents data and interprets information received from several hundred banks grouped by deposits (under $50 million; $50-200 million; over $200 million). Shows gross earnings, major expense categories and net earnings on income-producing functions.
2. Performance Characteristics of High-Earning Banks	Federal Reserve Board (annually)	Shows performance data for 25 percent of banks with the highest earnings. Contains seven size category groups from under $20 million to over $400 million.
3. Operating Ratios	Federal Reserve District Bank (annually)	Contains data on banks under each Reserve Bank's jurisdiction. Presents raw data to make the information more comparable with other banks. The information is reported by state and, in some cases, by metropolitan and non-metroplitan areas.

4. Bank Operating Statistics	Federal Deposit Insurance Corporation (annually)	Has five tables on designated economic areas within each state. 1. Assets and Liabilities, and Capital Accounts 2. Selected Balance Sheet Ratios 3. Income and Expenses by Area 4. Income and Expenses as a Percentage of Total Operating Revenue 5. Selected Operating Ratios
5. National Bank Surveillance System Report	Office of the Comptroller of the Currency (quarterly)	Compares individual bank performance to selected peer group. Contains significant ratios derived from call reports.

In using the reports listed in Table 4 to compare the bank's performance with that of other banks, consider that bank operating ratios tend to be quantitative, not qualitative. Many banks falling within a size category may have very different characteristics from the average bank in the group. Specifically, the bank may be urban, suburban, or rural, or be in a rapidly growing or declining economic environment. It may be the only bank in town or face strong competition from other banks, savings and loans, and credit unions. Therefore, as a measurement guide, ratios should be examined in light of their thrust or direction over time. Adverse trends in operating ratios should be given close attention, but sufficient information is needed to identify the reasons for the trends before sound corrective action can be taken.

NOTES FOR PART II

1. 12 U.S.C. §712
2. 12 U.S.C. §76
3. 12 U.S.C. §72
4. 12 U.S.C. §72
5. 12 U.S.C. §73

 6. Executive Order 11246, as amended
 7. 12 U.S.C. 2901, et. seq.
 8. See 12 C.F.R. 25.1, et seq.
 9. 12 C.F.R. 9.1 et. seq.
10. P.L. 93–406, Sept. 2, 1974
11. Civil Rights Act of 1964, Title VII
12. EEOC Guidelines, Part 1607
13. Fair Labor Standards Act of 1938, as amended; Age Discrimination in Employment Act of 1967; Portal-to-Portal Act of 1947; Equal Pay Act of 1963.
14. P.L. 93–406, Sept. 2, 1974
15. 12 U.S.C. §1881 ff.

PART III:

Directors' Legal Responsibilities and Liabilities

Reference has been made throughout this text to the legal duties of the bank director. This section will now concentrate more fully upon the nature and scope of the director's legal responsibilites and liabilities. This overview of the bank director's job does not allow for an exhaustive study of every possible area of legal concern, but it does highlight the major provisions of the federal law. The bank's legal counsel should be consulted for clarification and expansion of the basic information provided here.

The responsibilities and liabilities of bank directors are imposed by *common law, statutory law, securities law, antitrust law,* and *criminal law.* The basic responsibilities and liabilities of directors within these categories of law will be explained in this part. In all instances, the laws may vary somewhat, depending upon the state in which your bank is located, whether your bank is a national or state bank, and whether or not your bank is insured by the Federal Deposit Insurance Corporation. For convenience and clarity, this discussion will rely basically upon federal laws in the area. Be mindful that state law may supplement federal law or carry different penalties.

In addition to the discussion of the various categories of law and their implications in terms of directors' duties and liabilities, this part explains the various enforcement actions and procedures of the federal regulatory agencies: the Comptroller of the Currency, the Federal Reserve Board, and the Federal

Deposit Insurance Corporation (FDIC). Insurance and indemnification for directors are also discussed. Finally, some general guidelines are provided to help directors avoid potential liability in the fulfillment of their duties.

9
Common Law

Common law or "case law" is made by judicial decision rather than by legislation. It imposes duties upon directors in addition to those described in banking statutes. Under common law, all corporate directors, including bank directors, bear personal liability to their corporate shareholders for directing and supervising the corporation in the shareholders' best interests.

Common law defines standards of conduct for directors by describing the duties of directors in broad, basic terms. These general duties are not subject to any detailed or comprehensive definition, but are variously described as a duty of ordinary care, a duty to act as a prudent and reasonable person, and a duty to show loyalty and good faith.[1] Common law liability is determined by applying these general principles to the specific facts of each individual case. If a court finds that a director had such a duty to a particular person, did not fulfill that duty, and that the person to whom the duty was owed was damaged as a result of this failure, then the court will hold the director liable to that person.[2]

ORDINARY CARE AND PRUDENCE

The Supreme Court summarized the common law liability of bank directors in an 1891 case. The opinion in this case held that it is the director's duty to use ordinary diligence in ascertaining the condition of the bank, and to provide reasonable control and supervision of the bank's affairs. The opinion points out that a bank director is not expected to ensure the trustworthiness of each and every bank officer and employee, and that the director is not responsible for losses resulting from wrongful acts or omissions of others, unless these misdeeds were allowed to occur because the director failed to supervise the business as any prudent and reasonable person would.[3]

In another landmark case in 1899, the court, citing the rule of ordinary care, skill, and diligence, said:

> Under this rule, it is necessary for . . . (directors) to give the business under their care such attention as an ordinary discreet man would give to his own concerns under similar circumstances, and it is therefore incumbent upon them to devote so much of their time to their trust as is necessary to familiarize them with the business of the institution, and to supervise and direct its operations.[4]

In this case, the court found that the directors were personally liable to the bank's shareholders and creditors for losses caused by executive mismanagement. The directors' defense was that they had appointed executive officers of reported honesty and in whom they had confidence, and that the responsibility of managing and supervising the bank then shifted to those officers. But the court found that the directors had not fulfilled their duties to direct and supervise bank management. In its decision against the directors, the court said:

> The directors were not mere ornaments to the bank to lure public confidence. When they became directors, the law cast upon them the important duties of supervision and direction, which they could not delegate to the executive officers; and therefore the stockholders and depositors had the right to intrust the institution with their money, in confidence that the directors would perform those duties. When sued for losses which resulted from careless or unlawful acts and unfortunate transactions, they can never set up as a defense that they did not examine the books or accounts of the bank, knew nothing about the loans or discounts, were ignorant of

banking business, or that they intrusted the management and supervision of the business to the executive officers, in whom they had confidence. The welfare of the public and the interests of banking institutions alike forbid this.[5]

The opinion that directors are not insurers of the bank was upheld in a case determining whether or not directors had violated their duties of ordinary care and diligence. In this case, the forgery schemes of the chief executive officer led to the failure of the bank. The FDIC and the insurance company sued the directors. The court found that the loss must lie with the CEO, because the directors had been active and diligent in attending board meetings, reviewing loan applications, conducting outside audits, and following the advice of auditors, the FDIC, and the state banking authority. The court found that the directors had fulfilled their responsibility to exercise ordinary care. In its decision for the directors, the court stated that directors may properly rely on the honesty and integrity of officers and fellow directors ". . . until dishonest, unlawful and deceitful acts become obvious to the ordinary prudent bank . . . director."[6]

Common law defines ordinary care as "the degree of care which ordinarily prudent and diligent men would exercise under similar circumstances."[7] While bank directors are performing their ordinary duties, ordinary care is sufficient. Directors are not expected to spend all of their time or energy in a scrupulous overseeing of the day-to-day activities of the bank, since that is management's job. If nothing occurs to awaken the director's suspicions, no unusual responsibilities are required. However, if facts come to the director's attention that would cause any reasonable person to believe that something was out of line, then the director has an obligation to exercise "a degree of care commensurate with the evil to be avoided."[8]

The degree of care required depends on the specific circumstances of each case, and liability is largely determined based on the facts that directors knew or should have had cause to know at the time. Directors are not necessarily liable for losses due to bad judgment if they have exercised ordinary care; but directors can be held personally liable for violating their duty of ordinary care if they fail to take action when facts become apparent that would put a reasonable person on guard.[9]

Negligence on the part of directors is not enough for personal liability under statutory law, but it is under common law. The court has stated that directors who do not attend board meetings or who do so only infrequently can be held liable to a third party for losses resulting from their negligence.[10]

In some instances, directors who fail to meet the responsibilities imposed on them by statutory law also may be held personally liable for violations of their common law duty to the bank's shareholders. Directors must have a basic understanding of how the bank conducts business, and they should be familiar with capital requirements, loan controls, and collateral for larger loans.[11] Both statutory law and common law require that directors see that sound loan and investment policy is established and followed by management.[12] Failure to maintain adequate audit procedures is a violation of banking statutes as well as a violation of the director's common law duty to stay informed of the bank's financial condition.[13]

The American Bar Association's Committee on Corporate Laws has stated that, "given its widespread use, the absence of an audit committee may become a consideration in weighing whether directors of a publicly-held corporation have met the standard of care set forth in many of the state corporation laws."[14] In addition to complying with the recommendations of regulatory examiners, directors are expected to conduct their own examinations and audits, and to take any necessary action that may be indicated by their findings.

LOYALTY AND GOOD FAITH

Aside from the duty to do one's job as a director carefully and completely, common law also imposes a duty of loyalty upon bank directors. This enables parties harmed by a director's self-dealings to recover their damages from the director. For example, in one case, a bank director accepted gratuities for himself and his family from a group of the bank's borrowers. Because of these interests, he made certain that the borrowers received favorable treatment from the bank. The loans were not repaid, and the bank suffered as a result. As a violation against the criminal laws, such activity could subject the director to fines and imprisonment; but, in and of itself, that would do nothing for the bank or its stockholders—the National Bank Act had not been violated, so the damaged parties could not sue under that act. The court, however, did permit the bank to recover from the director the value of the gratuities because of his common law "breach of trust."[15]

Loyalty to the bank is usually defined as acting in good faith. Directors have a legal responsibility to disclose any conflicts of interest, to act in the best interests of the bank, to be fair in all corporate dealings, and to avoid self-interest or any interests that would be competitive or harmful to the bank.[16] Case law shows a variety of violations of the duty of loyalty, such as improper or self-serving loans, appropriation of corporate opportunity, and excessive compensation.[17]

In 1978, Congress passed the Financial Institutions Regulatory and Interest Rate Control Act (FIRA), which prescribes specific standards for insider transactions, in order to curb suspected abuses by directors and other insiders who might use their positions within the bank to advance their own interests.[18] This legislation will be discussed in Chapter 10 on statutory law. It should be noted here, however, that the common law duty of loyalty and good faith requires something more than the mere observance of the letter of these statutory requirements; as a trustee, the bank director is expected to observe an impeccably precise code of personal and business ethics.[19] The best rule of conduct is to avoid any activity that could not bear public disclosure.

10

Statutory Law

Under common law, a bank director has essentially the same corporate responsibilities as any other corporate director. In addition, a bank director is legally responsible for seeing that federal and state banking statutes are followed.[20] Bank statutory law encompasses a great many regulations, and directors are expected to be generally familiar with these legal requirements. Directors are presumed to know the law, and will be held accountable for any statutory violations.

PERSONAL LIABILITY

A director who violates or allows a violation of the law can be sued for damages by anyone harmed by the actions. The stockholders of the bank can sue the directors,[21] the insurance company that provides a bank's "blanket bond" can recover from the directors any payments it is required to make,[22] and a bank's depositors are entitled to recover damages as well, provided, of course, that they can prove a knowing violation of the law.[23] If insolvency of a bank occurs, the receiver, usually the Federal Deposit Insurance Corporation (FDIC), is also entitled to recover from the directors for any damages resulting from the breach of fiduciary responsibilities, as well as from the knowing violation of the laws. The power to pursue breach of fiduciary duty claims as the receiver of a failed institution "is, in effect, an additional enforcement tool at the disposal of the FDIC . . . and it is especially valuable in those cases of misconduct that do not present a strong basis for statutory enforcement proceedings."[24]

KNOWLEDGE AND INTENT IN VIOLATIONS

Perhaps the most useful starting point in a discussion of statutory law and director liability is Section 53 of the Naional Bank Act,[25] which was originally passed by the Congress in 1864 and has remained substantially unchanged except for specifying the civil penalty assessment for violations. Corresponding provisions in the law also relate to banks other than national banks.

Section 53 provides that if the directors of a national bank *knowingly* violate or knowingly *permit* the officers or employees of the bank to violate any of the other provisions of the act,[26] every director who participated in the violation or consented to it shall be liable, personally and individually, for any damages resulting from the violation, whether the damages are to the bank itself, its shareholders, or any other person.

The word "knowingly" is of particular importance. Obviously, if a bank director is fully aware of what he is doing, and intends to do something that is a violation of the law, there is no question that he can be held liable for damages resulting from his actions. However, the courts have not limited the word to that meaning. Liability will also be imposed on a bank director for "knowingly" permitting a law to be violated "if he deliberately refrained from investigating that which it was his duty to investigate."[27]

In one case, the directors of a bank were so sadly neglectful of their duties that the court held that they "knowingly" violated the law, even though they did so without any real knowledge. The bank had been victimized by an embezzlement, which the bank's internal audit procedures had failed to disclose. When this fact was eventually discovered, the directors took no action to correct the obvious deficiencies in the audit procedures. Some years later, another embezzlement took place. The directors appointed four employees of the bank to conduct an audit, and the employees reported that the losses were in the neighborhood of $80,000. Relying upon this information, the directors proceeded to declare a dividend for the bank's stockholders, since the bank showed a profit even after the $80,000 in embezzlement losses had been deducted. It was later discovered, first, that the losses were really $359,000; second, that two of the investigators appointed by the directors were themselves embezzlers; and third, that the bank showed an overall loss rather than a profit for the year.

In this case, the directors were found liable for civil damages since they had violated the law forbidding a national bank to pay dividends in excess of profits, and they had done so knowingly. Under the circumstances, they should have known and, in fact, had an obligation to know that the audit procedures were inadequate.[28] Ignorance is no excuse because the directors have a duty to know.

In a 1982 case, the court held that "directors of a national bank operate in an area closely regulated by federal law, and cannot maintain ignorance of the law as a defense."[29] The case dealt with three separate loans made by a California national bank to a corporation, its president, and the treasurer. The issue was whether the loans were really all to the corporation and, in the aggregate, violated the bank's legal lending limits. The court ruled that the monies were used collectively for the corporation and did violate the limits under 12 U.S.C. §84 (10 percent of the bank's capital stock to a single borrower). The directors argued, unsuccessfully, that they had no knowledge of the laws governing such loans.

However, in another similar case, the court held that the directors were not liable for damages. (This case was discussed in the previous section in the context of the common law opinion that directors are not insurers of the bank.) Here, the president of the bank had been committing forgeries and was embezzling from the bank. Before his offenses were discovered, he had been a highly respected member of the community, and there was no conceivable reason why the directors should have suspected him of anything. Also, a series of independent audits by highly qualified certified public accountants had failed to disclose anything wrong. Examinations by state and federal authorities had revealed several minor and unrelated problems with respect to the operation of the bank, and, without fail, the directors had moved to correct these deficiencies. None of the directors, except the president himself, had participated in the forgeries or the frauds. Under these circumstances, the court felt that the directors had properly and carefully carried out their duties. They could not be said to have "knowingly" permitted violations of the law.[30]

MAJOR STATUTORY REQUIREMENTS

Bank statutory law covers a wide range of subjects, and a complete survey of these regulations is beyond the scope of this text. Directors should consult with their bank's legal counsel to familiarize themselves with the full range of statutory requirements.

Only the most significant statutory requirements are discussed here, and it should be noted that this discussion relies basically upon federal laws in the area. Directors of state banks should understand that state banking statutes vary from state to state. While state statutes are similar to national statutes, directors of state-chartered banks should be thoroughly familiar with the laws governing banks in their particular state.

Examples of civil liability arising from violations of bank statutory laws that caused damage to others are discussed in the following sections.

Loans

A section of the National Bank Act 12 U.S.C. §84, forbids a national bank to make loans to any one entity that exceed 15 percent of the gross capital of the bank. (There are some exceptions to this law and reference to 12 U.S.C. §84 is recommended for further detailed information).[31] (Gross capital is generally computed by totalling capital, surplus, undivided profits, and 50 percent of reserves for loan losses. If the bank has preferred stock or other kinds of capital, that also would be included in the computation of gross capital.)

In one case, the directors of a bank knowingly made or permitted such loans, which were not repaid. As a result, the bank became insolvent. The minority stockholders of the bank were permitted to sue the directors to recover the damages they suffered when the value of their bank stock diminished because of the insolvency. The shareholders demonstrated that the directors knowingly violated 12 U.S.C. §84 and that the shareholders unknowingly relied on false reports.[32]

The 10 percent ratio applies at the point when the loan is made, not at the point of commitment to the loan. This means that directors must be regularly and continually aware of the bank's capital stock and surplus as defined by regulation (subordinated capital notes are included in the regulatory definition of capital stock plus surplus.) If a loan exceeds the required limits and a loss to the bank is sustained, the directors can be held liable for the full amount of the loan plus interest (less any recovery on the loan), not simply the amount of the loan over the 10 or 15 percent ratio.[33]

Banking statutes also cover loan collateral. A bank cannot make loans on the security of its capital stock.[34] Usually this statute is violated, not when the bank makes a direct loan, but when it participates in the making of a loan; information on collateral provided by the originating bank may be erroneous or it may not be reviewed by the participating bank. In a related area, the Federal Reserve prescribes value restrictions on bank loans secured by stock that are used to purchase stock "on margin."[35]

Real estate loans must conform to specific conditions set forth in the act, including the ratio of the loan to property value, lien requirements, loan guarantee requirements, and so on.[36]

The Federal Reserve Board's Regulation O covers loans by member banks to officers, directors, and stockholders and was amended December 31, 1983.[37] Regulation O now authorizes a member bank to extend credit to any executive officer of the bank in any amount to finance the education of the executive officer's children; in any amount to finance the purchase, construction, maintenance, or improvement of a residence of the executive officer, if the extension of credit is secured by a first lien on the residence and the residence is owned (or expected to be owned after the extension of credit) by the executive officer;

and for any other purpose if the aggregate amount of all loans to the officer does not exceed, at any one time, the higher of 2.5 percent of the bank's capital and unimpaired surplus or $25,000, but in no event more than $100,000.[38]

Interest on Director Deposits

The National Bank Act prohibits banks from paying more interest on director deposits than is paid on similar deposits of nondirectors. The key word in this statute is "similar." The terms, conditions, and amounts of director deposits may make these deposits more valuable to the bank than other deposits, and, in such cases, the deposits are not considered similar and greater interest may be paid.[39]

False Reports

Another section of federal law[40] requires that certain reports concerning the condition of the bank be made under oath. False reports are prohibited.[41] In one case, a false report was knowingly made, and investors relied upon the report in making a decision to purchase shares of stock in the bank. When the true condition of the bank became known, the value of the shares diminished. The investors were permitted to sue the offending bankers for losses.[42]

Intentional falsification of reports and records also can lead to fines against the bank's administrators.[43] In addition, banks are expected to provide accurate information in their required reports, and to submit these reports in a timely manner. Fines also may be levied by the FDIC against banks whose reports show gross errors or who continually file late reports.

Improper Payment of Dividends

Banks are prohibited from making improper payments of dividends. Dividends can be paid only from the bank's net profits, and only 90 percent of the bank's net profits can be paid as dividends until capital is equalled by surplus.[44]

Adhering to this provision may sometimes result in a decrease or interruption in dividend payments to shareholders, which directors would like to avoid. But the possibility of displeasing shareholders should not lead directors to consider violating this provision.[45] Doing so, in an attempt to provide consistent dividend payments, can endanger the financial stability of the bank.

Bank Premises

Banks are prohibited from making investments in bank premises or bank real estate if such investments exceed the bank's outstanding capital stock.[46] This prohibition is designed to restrict banks from overspeculation in real estate, and to discourage banks from jeopardizing their financial condition by investing in buildings of a size that far exceeds their needs.

Interest on Demand Deposits

Under federal law, direct payment of interest on demand deposits is prohibited. However, with the advent of NOW accounts, automatic transfers from savings accounts, and other innovations, banks are paying interest on deposits that approximate demand deposits in all but name. Limitations on the amount of interest that most banks can pay on various types of deposits[47] are being phased out.

Community Reinvestment

Another area of statutory law of importance to directors is the Community Reinvestment Act of 1977 (CRA).[48] The CRA requires that banks attempt to discover and meet the credit needs of their local communities. A bank's record of performance in meeting the credit needs of all segments of its community is considered by regulatory agencies when approving applications for branch expansion, mergers, and consolidations, the formation of bank holding companies, and so forth. If it is clear that a bank has not followed CRA regulations, the bank's application can be denied, probably leading to the loss of a valuable business opportunity for the bank. This could make the bank's directors liable to the shareholders for a breach of duty under common law.

Under the rules of the CRA, directors are required to see that a bank delineates all of the neighborhoods in its operating community. The board then must adopt a CRA Statement for each identified community, telling what types of credit the bank will offer in that community. The board of directors must annually review the bank's community delineation and its CRA Statements. Regulatory examiners look for accuracy and thoroughness in these materials when assessing the bank's performance record in meeting community credit needs.

Insider Transactions

Another very important area of bank regulation is that involving insider transactions. In 1978, Congress passed the Financial Institutions Regulatory and Interest Rate Control Act (FIRA),[49] which significantly increased the number and detail of legal statutes pertaining to a director's duties and liabilities regarding insider transactions.

FIRA was prompted by public concern that bank officials might use their positions as "insiders" to their personal advantage and at the expense of the bank. Although a few widely publicized cases of such insider abuse in the 1970s gave rise to this public concern, bank regulators had already been attentive to the possibility of such abuses and had recommended legislation to Congress.

The passage of FIRA provided legal prohibitions against insider abuse by detailing new duties for directors; duties which, if violated, can lead to director liability. FIRA also provided expanded supervisory powers and new enforcement procedures to bank regulatory agencies.

FIRA is composed of 21 sections or titles. Those titles that apply particularly to the duties and liabilities of directors are discussed here. It should be noted that most sections of FIRA define "insiders" as executive officers, directors, 10 percent shareholders of bank stock, any companies controlled by such persons, and any political or campaign committees controlled by or benefitting such persons. The act must be read carefully, however, because some sections do not define directors as insiders if they are not executive officers or 10 percent shareholders.[50]

- *Loan Requirements.* FIRA sets forth three major restrictions on loans to insiders. First, banks may not make preferential loans to directors, executive officers, 10 percent shareholders, or to any companies and campaign committees controlled by or benefitting insiders.[51] Loans to insiders must be treated in the same manner as comparable transactions with any other borrowers, with the same terms, interest rates, and collateral requirements, and with no more than the normal risk of repayment. Sometimes it can be argued that an apprarently preferential loan has special aspects that are not comparable to other transactions and that justify more favorable treatment. For the most part, however, directors should expect that their business dealings with the bank will be carefully scrutinized by the regulatory agencies, especially if the director plays a major role in the bank or controls any company that also does business with the bank.

  Second, FIRA requires that any loans to directors and other insiders totalling over an aggregate amount set by bank regulators must be approved in advance by the entire board (the amount is currently $25,000).[52] Advance lines of credit may be approved, but loans against such credit must be drawn within 14 months.

  The third restriction limits loans made to executive officers and 10 percent shareholders and their companies and campaign committees to an aggregate of not more than 15 percent of the bank's capital and surplus for loans not fully secured (10 percent for fully secured loans).[53] This restriction does not apply to directors who are not executive officers or 10 percent shareholders.

James Sexton, director, bank supervision, FDIC, advises bank directors to "limit and place high standards on insider credit. The bank's directors should be among the bank's best customers. In both volume and capacity, the credit of insiders should be totally circumspect and beyond criticism."[54]

Any violation of these insider lending limits can be penalized with a fine of up to $1,000 for each day the violation continues. Such civil money penalties can be made against the bank and any of its directors, officers, employees, agents, or other persons who participate in the conduct of the bank's affairs.

- *Disclosure of Insider Loans.* FIRA requires that banks submit annual reports listing all executive officers and any stockholders who own, control, or vote more than 10 percent of any class of the bank's voting securities.[55] The bank must also report the aggregate credit amounts outstanding to such persons and to the companies they control and the campaign committees they control or benefit from.

- *Overdrafts.* Banks are prohibited from allowing overdrafts for their directors and executive officers.[56] Written, prearranged automatic transfers of credit and preauthorized interest-bearing extensions of credit are exempted.[57] Inadvertent overdrafts of $1,000 or less are also exempted if paid within five business days and charged the usual customer fee.

- *Interlocking Directorates.* FIRA sets forth three basic restrictions on interlocking directorates.[58] First, "management officials" (including advisory or honorary directors) are prohibited from serving as management officials in other unaffiliated depository institutions (or depository holding companies) if the offices of both institutions (or their affiliates) are located within the same standard metropolitan statistical area or within the same, contiguous, or adjacent city, town, or village.

  Second, if both depository institutions have less than $20 million in assets, such interlocks are permitted within standard metropolitan statistical areas, but not if both institutions are located within the same, contiguous, or adjacent city, town, or village.

Third, management officials of a depository institution or holding company with more than $1 billion in assets are prohibited from serving as management officials of any unaffiliated depository institution with assets over $500 million.

These restrictions on interlocks are designed to preserve competition among depository institutions whose traditional differences are becoming less distinct. (Under FIRA, the definition of depository institution includes commercial banks, savings banks, cooperative banks, industrial banks, credit unions, savings and loans, building and loans, homestead associations, and trust companies.)[59]

There are some limited exceptions to the three restrictions on interlocks.[60] Interlocks are permitted in chain banking situations where both institutions are under common control because the same individual(s) holds 50 percent or more of the stock of both institutions. Interlocks are also permitted between a holding company and its subsidiary, or among subsidiaries of the same parent company. In addition, some limited operation or special purpose banks and trust companies are allowed interlocks with other banks or trust companies. Interlocks that existed before FIRA was enacted may continue through 1988. Illegal interlocks resulting from mergers or other voluntary arrangements that change ownership patterns are allowed a 15-month transition period for compliance.

- *Correspondent Relationships.* FIRA prohibits the making of preferential loans to a director, executive officer, or 10 percent shareholder of another bank that has a correspondent account relationship with the lending bank.[61] A correspondent account is an account maintained by a bank with another bank for the deposit or placement of funds.[62] This prohibition addresses the problem of a larger bank making a preferential loan to an insider who can influence his or her own bank to establish a correspondent relationship with the lending bank. Loans to insiders are permissible under such circumstances, but they must be made on the same terms as any other comparable transaction.

  This prohibition is designed to curb possible abuses in which an insider might direct his or her bank to deposit with another bank more funds than needed to secure correspondent services; in return, the insider gets preferential treatment on his or her loan from the bank receiving the excess correspondent deposits.

Both the bank making the preferential loan and the insider(s) participating in the loan transaction are bound by this prohibition, and they can be fined $1,000 a day for violations. Directors, executive officers, and 10 percent shareholders must report to the board in writing any credit received from another bank that has a correspondent relationship with their own bank. The board must forward this information to the bank's federal regulatory agency.

- *Expanded Powers of Regulatory Agencies.* Title I greatly increases the ability of federal bank regulatory agencies to enforce the provisions of FIRA. Specifically, the agencies have expanded powers to invoke civil money penalties, to issue cease and desist orders against individuals (making the individual liable to monetary fines), and to remove officers and directors who show a willful disregard for the bank's safety. These and other enforcement actions and procedures of federal bank regulatory agencies are discussed in Chapter 13.

- *Additional Provisions.* Directors should be aware of other important legal provisions of FIRA that deal with changes in bank control,[63] the protection of consumers who use electronic funds transfer services,[64] and the consumer's right to financial privacy.[65] Directors should carefully read these sections of FIRA as well as the sections covering the major provisions discussed in this text. Any questions on director responsibilities should be directed to the bank's legal counsel.

Other Statutory Requirements

The statutory requirements just discussed are only some of the major provisions of a great body of bank regulation. Additional statutes cover standards for security procedures and devices; specific terminology used in bank titles ("national," "national association," "N.A.") and in bank advertising ("FDIC-insured"); types of bank advertising allowed; the value of promotional premiums given to depositors; limitations on indebtedness for national banks; and disclosure of information to shareholders,[66] among other areas.

11

Securities and Antitrust Law

The Securities Exchange Act of 1934 created the Securities Exchange Commission (SEC) to administer statutes for the protection of the investing public against malpractice in the securities and financial markets. Banks were originally exempt from the act, but now any bank with more than 500 shareholders and more than $1 million in assets falls under its reach.[67]

The act requires that bank regulatory agencies prescribe and enforce regulations to carry out its provisions. Bank directors may be liable at common law for using the proceeds of a securities offering for purposes other than that approved by board resolution.[68]

The basic thrust of the securities laws is full disclosure of pertinent information. Specific prohibitions include fraud, deceptive or manipulative practices, misusing insider information, misrepresentations, and failure to disclose significant or material facts. Violations of the securities laws can lead to penalties of up to $5,000 and five years in prison. Civil liability for a bank director also may arise from violations of the securities laws, if damages can be proved.

In recent years, violations of the antifraud provisions[69] of the securities laws have become more prevalent. Although banks do not ordinarily deal in securities on their own account, this fact does not exempt banks or their directors from the provisions of the law in all cases. In one case, several directors of a bank devised a scheme of artificially inflating certain stock prices by purchasing large quantities of the stocks but not paying for them immediately. Settlement drafts to cover the cost of these securities were directed to the bank for payment, and directors used their position with the bank to delay payment of the drafts. The sellers and brokers were told that payment was unavoidably delayed or that payment was in progress, when, in fact, these statements were untrue. By the time settlement was made, the stocks would have increased in value, been sold for a profit, and the proceeds used to make the settlement. The sellers were permitted to sue both the directors and the bank for violation of the law prohibiting the making of any false statement in connection with the purchase and sale of securities, and for common law fraud.[70]

Directors should make sure that no misrepresentations are made concerning the bank, including the omission of material facts. Material facts are those that any reasonable investor would consider significant. For example, in one case, a borrower wanted a loan in the amount of $325,000 from a particular bank. The bank was unable to make the loan, because it would have exceeded the 10 percent loan limitation prescribed by law at that time. Therefore, the bank sold a participation in the loan to a second bank and assured the second bank that the borrowers were financially sound. The loan was not repaid, and the second bank sued the first, charging common law fraud and violation of the law prohibiting anyone from failing to reveal a material fact in connection with the purchase or sale of securities. The second bank successfully argued that the sale of a participation in a loan was a security within the meaning of the law.

There were also several material facts omitted at the time of the transaction. The first bank had neglected to disclose its difficulties in collecting past loans to the same borrowers, the fact that bank examiners had criticized the loans to these borrowers, the fact that other banks, known to the first bank, had been required to foreclose on loans they had made to the borrowers, that these foreclosures had impaired the property used to secure the $325,000 loan in question, and that the borrowers had reported having an "extremely bad year" to the first bank.[71]

James Sexton of the FDIC has advice concerning loan participations:

When buying loan participations from another bank, assume that the selling bank will not repurchase them. Loans are sometimes sold under a tacit (but unwritten) repurchase agreement. The purchasing bank, by relying on the seller to backstop credit problems in the participation, is at risk not only for its own loan risks, but those of the seller. Simply stated, if the purchasing bank is relying on the purchase agreement, either implied or written, as a proxy for credit quality, the loans should not have been purchased.[72]

Another case involved a large national bank serving as executor of an estate of a majority stockholder in a small corporation. When all assets of the corporation were exchanged for stock in another corporation, a minority stockholder filed suit on behalf of the small corporation. He was able to demonstrate that the stock received in return for the assets was only about one-half as valuable as the assets, that the bank had failed to disclose this fact to the stockholders before the exchange, and that the bank had a conflict of interest in the transaction. The court found that this was a violation of the securities laws and permitted the minority stockholder to recover damages, not only from the bank itself, but also from the officers of the bank responsible for the transaction.[73]

Shares of stock in the bank itself are securities within the meaning of the law. They are specifically exempted from some of the requirements of the securities statutes relating to registration of the stock with the SEC.[74] Still, when the bank or its directors issue or sell the bank's own stock, the provisions of the law prohibiting fraud, misrepresentation, or failure to disclose material facts remain applicable.

Antitrust laws impose liability upon bank directors as well as on business persons at large. While banking, as a heavily regulated industry, enjoys a limited exemption from some antitrust laws, this fact does not protect directors or banks in all circumstances. For example, it is unlawful for anyone, including bank directors, to engage in a conspiracy in restraint of trade to fix prices, or to monopolize or attempt to monopolize any line of business. These laws may be enforced by the government, either civilly or criminally, or by individuals who may sue for three times the amount of the actual damages they suffer as a result of antitrust law violations.

The antitrust laws provide, specifically, that if a corporation violates any of the criminal provisions of the antitrust laws, the violation shall also be considered to have been a violation by the individual directors of the corporation who authorized or ordered the violation.[75]

12
Criminal Law

Among all the areas of legal responsibility of a bank director, conviction for a violation of the criminal laws is, of course, the most damaging thing that can occur. In almost all cases, a criminal *intent* is a necessary element of the offense.

This does not mean an intent to violate a specific statute, but rather an intent to carry out a specific act that is prohibited. For example, one section of the federal criminal code prescribes a penalty of a fine and a prison term for making "any false entry in any book, report, or statement" of any national, member, or insured bank. However, in order to violate this statute, the false entry must be made "with intent to injure or defraud" the bank.[76]

False entry can also occur if the offender was simply indifferent to the consequences of the false entry.[77] However, if a false entry is made solely due to negligence or carelessness, no crime has been committed, even if the bank suffers as a result. If damages can be proven, such negligence or carelessness may lead to civil, but not criminal, liability.

VIOLATIONS AND PENALTIES

Because violations of criminal law are intentional, their penalties are quite severe. Directors who knowingly or willfully commit a criminal act or omission can be held liable for penalties of up to $10,000 in fines and five years in prison, depending on the crime. Directors also can be suspended or removed if indicted for a felony involving dishonesty or breach of trust (conviction of the crime is not necessary for such suspension or removal). In addition to criminal penalties, violations of criminal laws may also give rise to civil liabilities.[78]

Examples of the major criminal law violations and their penalties are discussed in the following sections.

Misapplication of Bank Funds

Probably the most frequently prosecuted offense involving bank directors is the misapplication of the bank's funds or of funds entrusted to the bank. For any such misapplication over $100, the penalty can consist of a fine, a prison term, or both.[79] Once again, in order to commit this violation, the misapplication must be willful. An innocent misapplication is not a crime, but "reckless disregard by a bank official of his bank's interest is sufficient to establish the requisite intent to defraud."[80] Proof of personal gain is not a prerequisite to conviction, and the possibility of future benefits to the bank is not a defense to the charge of misapplication.[81]

Misapplication of funds can occur in a number of ways. In one case,[82] a bank director, who had no money in his account at the bank, but who nevertheless obtained money from the bank for his own use by means of an overdraft, was found guilty of this offense. In another case,[83] bank directors who illegally declared a dividend, intending to defraud the bank, were convicted of misapplication of funds. A recent case in Massachusetts[84] held that it is a criminal misapplication of funds for bank officials to grant loans knowingly to financially incapable parties. In 1979, *U.S. v. Twifold* held:

Defendant bank officers' self-dealing constituted willful misapplication of funds of a federally protected bank even though the borrower was capable of repaying the loan at the time it was made and he understood that he was solely liable for repayment.[85]

The same section of the criminal law also prohibits a director or anyone else connected with the bank from embezzling, abstracting, or purloining the bank's funds or funds in the custody of the bank.

Bribery and Graft

Another section of the criminal law sets a punishment of a prison term and a fine for bribery or graft. Specifically, it is illegal for any bank director to stipulate for, receive, or consent or agree to receive any fee, commission, gift, or anything else of value in return for procuring or even attempting to procure a loan, or influencing an important part of a loan transaction, on behalf of a prospective borrower.[86]

Improper Certification of Checks

It is also a criminal offense for a bank director improperly to certify a check before the face amount of the check has been deposited by the drawer of the check.[87]

False Advertising

It is unlawful for any bank to falsely advertise that it is a national bank, that it is insured by the Federal Deposit Insurance Corporation, or that it is a member of the Federal Reserve System. If this prohibition is violated, the bank itself may be fined up to $1,000, but more importantly, there is a personal criminal liability of up to one year in prison and a $1,000 fine for any officer of the bank participating in or knowingly acquiescing to the violation.[88]

Lotteries

Three separate sections of the banking laws prohibit participation by banks in lotteries. Section 9–A[89] of the

Federal Reserve Act applies this prohibition to state member banks of the Federal Reserve; Section 20[90] of the Federal Deposit Insurance Act applies it to state nonmember insured banks; and an amendment to the National Bank Act[91] applies it to national banks. The prohibition is a pervasive one. Not only are banks forbidden to participate in lotteries in the sense of buying, selling, or redeeming lottery tickets, but they are even forbidden to advertise the existence of a lottery or publicize the names of winners.

Once again, there is a personal criminal liability attached to any individual who knowingly violates this law, with a possible punishment of a prison term and a fine.[92] These sections of the law, however, do not prevent a bank from performing normal banking services, such as accepting deposits or cashing checks in the usual course of business for a state operating a lottery.

Political Activities

Another area of much current interest concerns political activities by banks. As a general rule, national banks are prohibited from making a contribution or expenditure in connection with election to any political office, including local, state, and federal offices. State banks are prohibited from making contributions or expenditures in connection with any federal election. However, in *National Bank of Boston et al. v. Bellotti*,[93] the court held that the contribution and expenditure prohibitions apply only to any candidate, committee, or political party in connection with an election, thus excluding referendum votes and constitutional amendments.

This rule, however, does not prevent a bank from making a loan to a candidate or party, as long as the loan is made in accordance with all relevant banking laws and done in the normal course of business. These limitations are placed upon banks so that they will not be able to make contributions in the guise of loans, simply to be written off as "bad debts" when the campaign is over.

The law also permits a bank or its trade association to establish a separate segregated fund to which stockholders, officers, and employees of the bank may make contributions for political purposes. There are numerous limitations and regulations governing the creation and operation of the separate funds authorized under the law, and compliance with the regulations is policed by the Federal Election Commission.

Of particular importance is the regulation that prohibits a bank director from consenting to any prohibited bank contribution.[94] Also, any person who knowingly and willfully commits a violation of the Federal Election Campaign Act, which involves the making, receiving, or reporting of any contribution or expenditure totalling $2,000 or more during a calendar year can be fined up to $25,000 or 300 percent of any contribution or expenditure, or imprisoned for up to one year, or both.[95]

Lending Funds Held in Trust

It is unlawful for a national bank to lend funds held in trust by the bank to any officer, director, or employee of the bank. A director or officer who makes or receives such a loan may face fines up to $5,000 and imprisonment up to five years.[96]

Loans or Gifts
to Bank Examiners

A bank director may be imprisoned for up to one year and fined $5,000 plus the amount of loan or gratuity for making a loan or gift of money to a bank examiner.[97] These penalties are applicable to any bank insured by the Federal Deposit Insurance Corporation and to any public examiner, that is, an examiner appointed by the federal or state government. It is not applicable to private examiners hired by a clearinghouse or by the directors themselves.

13

Regulatory Enforcement Actions and Procedures

Banking is one of the most heavily regulated industries in America, and certainly one of the most closely and consistently scrutinized. All banks are subject to periodic in-depth examinations by federal and state authorities to insure compliance with bank regulations and to identify any problems that may exist with respect to the bank's operations.

Such examinations are not regularly scheduled and do not require advance notice, so directors must see that the bank is always prepared for close inspection. If any problems are alleged or identified in the bank examination, follow-up examinations are conducted. It is the duty of the board of directors to see that bank management immediately attempts to resolve or correct any questions raised by the bank's examiners in their examination report. In a 1979 case, the court held that "the duty to discover fraud in their institutions is upon bank directors, and they may not transfer it to the FDIC by the easy expedient of purchasing insurance protection from it."[98]

If such problems are not resolved or corrected, the regulatory agencies are empowered by law to take administrative actions against banks, directors, and officers under certain circumstances. The Comptroller of the Currency may act with respect to national banks, the Federal Reserve Board with respect to state member banks, and the Federal Deposit Insurance Corporation (FDIC) with respect to insured, nonmember banks.

These regulatory agencies and their examiners have a variety of legal actions and procedures to enforce correction and com-

127

pliance, some of which, as noted earlier, were expanded by the passage of the Financial Institutions Regulatory and Interest Rate Control Act (FIRA). The enforcement actions and procedures available to regulatory agencies include informal meetings and agreements, letters of agreement, cease and desist orders, civil penalties, director removal or suspension, and termination of insured status.[99]

INFORMAL MEETINGS AND AGREEMENTS

Most problems identified in bank examinations are resolved informally. The bank examiner discusses such problems with management. In addition, the examiner may call a meeting with the board to recommend an appropriate course of action for the bank. Board members should be familiar with the contents of the examiner's report, and be well-prepared to discuss the points raised by it. Board meetings called by examiners do not necessarily mean that the bank is faced with serious problems. Directors should view the examination report as a constructive guide and the examiner as a valuable resource who can clarify sometimes complicated details of regulatory compliance and alert the bank to potentially dangerous operating procedures. Informal arrangements may also take place between the board and the regulatory agency's regional or national offices.

LETTER AGREEMENTS

Letter agreements are sometimes used when an informal meeting with the board does not result in action by directors that the regulator deems sufficient. In a letter agreement, the board agrees to stop specified practices and to take the actions recommended by the agency. Letter agreements are less formal arrangements than cease and desist orders, but if they are violated, a cease and desist order or other enforcement procedure may follow.

CEASE AND DESIST ORDERS

Cease and desist orders are normally directed at a bank rather than specifically at the directors of the bank; however, since a bank acts through its directors and officers, the directors may well be bound by the order, and under the new provisions of FIRA, cease and desist orders can be directed to specifically named individuals.

Cease and desist proceedings may be started if a regulatory agency believes that a bank is violating any law, rule, or regulation, or that it is, or is about to, engage in any unsafe or unsound practice. A notice of cease and desist proceedings is sent to the bank, and a hearing is set to determine if the order should be issued. The agency may also deliver a copy of the charges to the bank. The defendants named in the order are then given 20 days to respond. Usually, the defendants are given an opportunity to consent to the cease and desist order and thereby avoid a public hearing. If a public hearing is held, the bank may appeal an adverse decision.

A temporary cease and desist order may be issued by the agency only in the event that failure to act immediately would likely result in severe damage to the bank. It is effective immediately upon delivery and can be appealed.

CIVIL MONEY PENALTIES

As noted earlier, the expanded powers given regulatory agencies under FIRA provide for civil money penalties against directors, officers, employees, agents, or other persons involved in the conduct of the bank's affairs, for violations of specific acts. Under FIRA, such persons also can be named in cease and desist orders, thereby becoming liable to fines of up to $1,000 a day.

Director Removal or Suspension

If a bank director is formally charged with the commission of a felony that involves personal dishonesty or breach of trust, the appropriate agency may suspend the director from office and prohibit his or her further participation in the affairs of the bank. This is accomplished simply by sending a notice to the director in question and to the bank. If the director is eventually convicted of the felony, the agency may remove the director from office if a determination is made that his or her continued participation may pose a threat to the interests of the bank's deposits or may threaten to impair public confidence in the bank. The judgment is not subject to further appellate review.[100] While there is no right to notice or hearing prior to suspension or removal after a felony conviction, the bank director may request an informal hearing after the agency acts on the conviction.[101]

If the director is acquitted of a felony charge, this fact alone does not prevent the agency from suspending or removing the director anyway, but that would have to be done after a formal hearing, and the action could be appealed.

Suspension or removal of a director from office may occur for reasons other than indictment for or conviction of a felony, but certain facts must be established before an agency can remove a bank director from office. First, the agency must be of the opinion that the director has done or omitted one of several specified activities. These include any violation of a law, rule, regulation, or final cease and desist order issued by the agency. The specified activities also include participation in any unsafe or unsound practice or breach of a fiduciary duty with respect to the bank. These are rather broad terms, of course, and are subject to interpretation by the agency or the courts. Second, in order to remove or suspend a director not convicted or indicted, the agency must determine that the activity in question will likely result in substantial loss or damage to the bank or its depositors.

If such facts can be established, proof of personal dishonesty is no longer required for director removal; under Title I of FIRA, any officer or director now can be removed who shows continuous willful disregard for the safety and soundness of the bank, or whose continued presence would threaten the safety and soundness of the bank.[102]

The first step toward complete removal of a bank director from office may be, but is not necessarily, his or her suspension. A director may be suspended by the appropriate agency if the agency believes that such a step is necessary for the protection of the bank or its depositors. The suspension is accomplished by delivery of a notice to the director in question and to the bank. It is effective immediately upon delivery, but it may be appealed.

TERMINATION OF INSURED STATUS

The FDIC is empowered under the Federal Deposit Insurance Act to notify a bank of the existence of unsafe or unsound practices by the bank or its directors, of unsound conditions within the bank, or of violations of laws and regulations or written agreements with the FDIC.[103] Upon such notification, the bank is given a period of from 20 to 120 days to correct the problems, after which the FDIC examines the bank. If it finds that the problems are not resolved by the time the correction period expires, it may notify the bank of its intent to terminate the bank's deposit insurance. Then it sets a hearing date.

If a final order terminating the bank's insurance is eventually entered, the results must be made public. No new deposits may be insured, although the bank's existing deposits remain insured for two years. The result of publication that the bank's deposit insurance has been terminated is usually bank failure. In the event of the failure of the bank, it is likely that the FDIC, as liquidator, will file suit against the directors for damages.

14

Insurance and Indemnification

All bank directors are subject to the risk of possible lawsuits. Even the most conscientious directors may be forced to defend themselves against allegations of breach of duty, however tenuous, made by shareholders not satisfied with the bank's performance or by third parties claiming they have suffered losses or damages as a result of the directors' negligence or misconduct. Even if such claims are settled in the directors' favor, the costs of litigation and defense can be enormous.

Since directors cannot be expected to bear the full risk of the costs of possible litigation, they are protected from liability through insurance and indemnification. Insurance protects the director from having to bear the full cost of defending and settling lawsuits. Indemnification protects the director from personal financial losses suffered as a result of his or her service as a director.

Indemnification of directors is governed by state statutes for banks with state charters and by guidelines of the Comptroller of the Currency for national banks. In general, indemnification protects a director from losses suffered as a result of third party suits if the director acted in good faith and in the best interests of the corporation; for derivative actions (suits filed by shareholders in the interests of the corporation), indemnification is not permitted if the director is found liable for negligence or misconduct.[104]

Insurance includes two basic types of coverage:

- directors' and officers' liability insurance covers directors and officers against actions for wrongful acts that cannot be indemnified;
- company reimbursement liability insurance protects the bank for claims against the director for acts that the bank is required or permitted to indemnify.

Directors should carefully examine the types of insurance and indemnification coverage provided by the bank. Moreover, they should consult with legal counsel to make sure that such protection is adequate and that it conforms to regulations set forth by the Comptroller of the Currency or to state banking statutes.

15

Some General
Guidelines for
Directors

      The role of the bank director has changed dramatically in recent years and, with it, so has the potential for substantial personal liability. A recent article in *The Business Lawyer* stresses that federal bank regulatory agencies have increased their enforcement of the law:

> . . . as a matter of statistical probability, officers, directors, and other insiders of a federally insured bank or thrift institution are more likely now than at any other time during the last half-century to find themselves the named defendants in civil or criminal actions initiated by a federal regulator.[105]

As a result of the recent increase in failed banks (75 FDIC-insured commercial banks between January 1, 1980, and May 17, 1983), a study was conducted by the House Subcommittee on Commerce, Consumer, and Monetary Affairs into the enforcement of criminal laws against bank officers, directors, and other insiders of "problem" financial institutions. The survey showed a high correlation between the number of failed commercial banks and "the incidence of actual or probable criminal misconduct by officers, directors, and insiders."[106] These facts show the need for bank directors to be fully prepared for their responsibilities and duties before taking office.

      Here are a few steps you should follow in carrying out your duties as a director:

1. *Familiarize yourself with your statutory, criminal, and common law responsibilities, both state and federal.* The

Comptroller of the Currency publishes a brochure entitled *Duties and Liabilities of Directors of National Banks*. This or similar literature might be helpful. In addition, ask your legal counsel to prepare a brief for you since the nature and specificity of legislation vary from state to state.

2. *Exercise reasonable diligence and common sense.* It is certainly reasonable to trust your officers, but directors' duty of care does not end once officers have been selected. There is also a duty of supervision. Furthermore, it is unreasonable not to check the books. If discrepancies or shortages are discovered, the explanations of trusted officers and employees will not save the directors from responsibility. You have a duty to inquire. If any irregularities or discrepancies arise concerning your bank, you are obligated to investigate them fully.

3. *Make sure your personal assets are insured.* Examine the bylaws of your bank for indemnification provisions, and seek insurance for exposures that are not indemnifiable.

4. *Exercise ordinary care and prudence.* Poor judgment is not considered lack of prudence. You are not legally liable for making an erroneous judgment if it was based on a sincere effort and if you exercised your duty to inquire. Lack of knowledge, however, can be a breach of duty. Care and prudence require you not to overlook any facts and not to fail to take some action on a known problem.

5. *Pay particular attention to the things the court will look at if your bank gets into trouble.* One way to prepare yourself against possible charges is to look at some of the records the court will requisition in deciding its case:

   • *The examination committee function over the last ten years.*
   The courts will want to know if the examination committee saw to it that the bank was examined at regular intervals, that there were no omissions in the examination, and that action was taken on suspected irregularities or whatever was indicated in the examination reports.

- *The dates and regularity of meetings.*
  Different state or national charters set requirements for the frequency of board meetings. The courts will look to see that at least the required minimum number of meetings was held.

- *Each director's attendance pattern.*
  Lack of attendance at board meetings can be considered negligence. Unawareness of an issue that was discussed in the director's absence does not necessarily exempt the director from liability.

- *The integration of management reports into the minutes.*
  The board's meeting minutes should indicate the nature and scope of management reports and the initiation of action where indicated.

- *The loan and discount committee activities.*
  The loan and discount committee is responsible for the approval and/or review of the bank's loans. Any illegal activity, failure to be alerted to potential trouble, or neglect may be detected from a review of these activities.

- *Abnormal fluctuations in savings and checking account totals.*
  A major loss of accounts could signify a loss of confidence in the bank or the loss of a major depositor. Fluctuations in the account totals that have gone uninvestigated may be questioned by the court.

- *The volume and nature of the loan and investment portfolios.*
  An investigation of the loan and investment portfolio may give evidence of unsound lending practices, speculative investments, or other irregularities.

- *Action taken on known or irregular acts of officers and employees.*
  If action has not been taken by the board regarding activities of officers and employees, or if such activities have not been detected, directors could be liable for negligence.

- *Evidence regarding officers who appear to be living beyond their means.*
  In event of bank loss or failure, officers, employees, or directors who appear to be living beyond their means may be suspected of criminal activity. If a director senses this situation, he or she is obligated to investigate, even though there may be no wrongdoing.

- *Evidence of self-dealing (preferential treatment not in the bank's best interest).*
  Directors can be held liable for any action, such as making loans, that is more in the interest of the recipient than the bank or the stockholders. In the wake of bank failures, due, in part, to risky loans, directors should be cautious in voting for substantial loans to borrowers outside of the local community.

6. *Do not be afraid to vote "no" when you disagree or to abstain from a vote involving a conflict of interest. Request that your vote be recorded.* Your voting record may be your best defense. If you have gone on record as opposing an action that later caused problems for the bank, you may not be held accountable.

The director who is diligent in exercising care and prudence in all banking matters and who pays attention to the foregoing points, will probably not be held liable. The FDIC's position is: "One who voluntarily takes the position of director undertakes that he possesses at least ordinary knowledge and skill and that he will bring them to bear in the discharge of his duties."

While the potential for personal liability has increased, the standards for directors have always been high. In a recent article on bank directors came a quote from an 1897 court decision:

What the public suppose, and have the right to suppose, is that those men [directors] have been selected by reason of their high character for integrity, their sound judgment, and their capacity for conducting the affairs of the bank safely and securely. The public act on this presumption, and trust their property with the bank in the confidence that the directors will discharge a substantial duty.[107]

A director need not fear making difficult or innovative decisions for the bank. By discharging his or her responsibilities with care and diligence and from a legally informed position, the director obtains the best protection against personal liability.

NOTES FOR PART III

1. Edwin B. Cox et al., *The Bank Director's Handbook* (Boston, Mass.: Auburn House Publishing Company, 1981), pp. 133–135.
2. *Bowerman v. Hamner*, 250 U.S. 504 (1919).
3. *Briggs v. Spaulding*, 141, U.S. 132 (1891).
4. *Warren v. Robinson*, 57 Pac. 287 (Utah, 1899).
5. Ibid.
6. *FDIC v. Boone*, 361 F. Supp. 133 (W.D. Okla., 1972).
7. *Briggs v. Spaulding*, 141 U.S. 132, 152 (1891).
8. *Rankin v. Cooper*, 149 Fed. 1010 (W.D. Ark., 1907).
9. Ibid.
10. *Bowerman v. Hamner*, op. cit.
11. *Briggs v. Spaulding*, op. cit.
12. *Corsicana National Bank v. Johnson*, 251 U.S. 68, 71 (1919); *Hughes v. Reed*, 46 Fed. 435 (10th Circ., 1931).
13. *Rankin v. Cooper*, op. cit.
14. Report, "The Overview Committees of the Board of Directors," 34 *Business Lawyer* 1837 (1979).
15. *First National Bank of Lincolnwood v. Keller*, 318 F. Supp. 339 (N.D. Ill., 1970).
16. Cox et al, p. 135.
17. Robert E. Barnett, *Responsibilities and Liabilities of Bank Directors* (Chicago, Ill.: Commerce Clearing House, Inc., 1980) pg. 26 [*Barber v. Kolowich*, 282 Mich. 143, 277 N.W. 189 (1938); *Meinhard v. Salmon*, 249 N.Y. 458, 164 N.E. 545 (1928); *Rogers v. Hill*, 289 U.S. 582 (1932)].
18. Financial Institutions Regulatory and Interest Rate Control Act of 1978, P.L. 95–630, 92 Stat. 3641 (Nov. 10, 1978).
19. *Meinhard v. Salmon*, 249 N.Y. 458, 164 N.E. 545 (1928).
20. 12 U.S.C. §93.
21. *First National Bank of Lincolnwood v. Keller*, op. cit.
22. *FDIC v. Boone*, op. cit.
23. *Hoehn v. Crews*, 144 F. 2d. 665 (10th Circ., 1944).
24. "Bank Officer and Director Liability — Regulatory Actions," 39 *The Business Lawyer* 1029 (1984).
25. 12 U.S.C. §93.
26. Chapter 2 of Title 12 U.S.C.
27. *Corsicana National Bank v. Johnson*, op. cit.

28. FDIC v. Mason, 115 F. 2d. 548 (3rd Circ., 1940).
29. del Junco v. Conover, C.A. 9, 1982, 682 F. 2d. 1338, cert. denied 103 S. Ct. 786 (1983).
30. FDIC v. Boone, op. cit.
31. 12 U.S.C. §84.
32. Harmsen v. Smith, 542 F. 2d. 496 (9th Circ., 1976).
33. Corsicana National Bank v. Johnson, op. cit.; Rankin v. Cooper, op. cit.; Gambell v. Brown, 29 F. 2d. 366 (4th Circ., 1928).
34. 12 U.S.C. §83.
35. 15 U.S.C. §78g(d).
36. 12 U.S.C. §371.
37. 12 U.S.C. §375(a).
38. Sections 215.5, 215.8, and 215.9 of Regulation O implementing section 22(g) of the Federal Reserve Act.
39. 12 U.S.C. §376.
40. 12 U.S.C. §161.
41. 18 U.S.C. §1005.
42. Cherbourgh v. Woodworth, 244 U.S. 72 (1917).
43. 18 U.S.C. §1005.
44. 12 U.S.C. §56, 60.
45. Barnett, p. 18.
46. 12 U.S.C. §371(d).
47. 12 U.S.C. §371(b), 1819, 1928.
48. 12 U.S.C. §2901, et. seq.
49. FIRA, P.L. 95–630.
50. Barnett, p. 29.
51. FIRA, Secs. 104(h) (3) and 108.
52. FIRA, Secs. 104(h) (2) and 108.
53. 12 U.S.C. §275b, 12 U.S.C. §84.
54. "Directors' Responsibility: Old and New," Southern Banker, July 83, p. 17.
55. FIRA, Title IX.
56. FIRA, Secs. 104(h) (4) and 108.
57. FIRA, Sec. 104(h) (5) (6).
58. FIRA, Secs. 203, 204.
59. Barnett, p. 34.
60. FIRA, Secs. 202(3) (b) and 203.
61. FIRA, Title VIII.
62. 12 U.S.C. §1972 (2) (a).
63. FIRA, Title VI.
64. FIRA, Title XX.
65. FIRA, Title XI.
66. Cox et al., p. 137.
67. Barnett, p. 42.
68. Emmert v. Drake, 224 F. 2d. 299 (5th Circ., 1955).
69. 15 U.S.C. §78j (b) and Rule 10(b) (5) of the Securities Exchange Commission.

70. *Carrol v. First National Bank of Lincolnwood*, 413 F. 2d. 353 (7th Circ., 1969).
71. *Lehigh Valley Trust Co. v. Central National Bank of Jacksonville*, 409 F. 2d. 989 (5th Circ., 1969).
72. *Southern Banker*, op. cit.
73. *Bailey v. Meister Brau*, 535 F. 2d. 982 (7th Circ., 1976).
74. 15 U.S.C. §77c.
75. 15 U.S.C. §24.
76. 18 U.S.C. §1005.
77. *U.S. v. McAnally*, C.A. Ill., 1981, 666 F. 2d. 116.
78. Barnett, p. 45.
79. 18 U.S.C. §656.
80. *U.S. v. Cyr.*, C.A. Mass., 1983, 712 F. 2d. 729.
81. See *Hernandez v. U.S.*, C.A. 12, 1979, 608 F. 2d. 1361, and *U.S. v. Beran*, C.A. N.D., 1976, 546 F. 2d. 1316, *cert. denied*, 430 U.S. 916.
82. *U.S. v. Warner*, 26 F. 616 (Circuit Court, New York, 1886).
83. *U.S. v. Matsinger*, 191 F. 2d. 1014 (3rd Circuit Court of Appeals, 1951).
84. *U.S. v. Gens*, 493 F. 2d. 216 (1st Circuit Court of Appeals, 1974).
85. *U.S. v. Twifold*, C.A. Colo., 1979, 600 F. 2d. 1339.
86. 18 U.S.C. §215.
87. 18 U.S.C. §1004.
88. 18 U.S.C. §709.
89. 12 U.S.C. §339.
90. 12 U.S.C. §1829a.
91. 12 U.S.C. §25a.
92. 18 U.S.C. §1306.
93. *National Bank of Boston et al. v. Bellotti*, 435 U.S. 765 (1978).
94. 11 C.F.R. §114.2(2) (d).
95. 2 U.S.C. §37g(d) (1) (6).
96. 12 U.S.C. §92a.
97. 18 U.S.C. §212.
98. *First State Bank of Hudson County v. U.S.*, 599 F. 2d. 558 (3rd. Circ., 1979), *cert. denied*, 444 U.S. 1013 (1980).
99. Barnett, pp. 47–61.
100. 12 U.S.C. §1818(g) (i).
101. 12 C.F.R., 263.32.
102. FIRA, Sec. 107.
103. 12 U.S.C. §1818(a).
104. Cox et al., pp. 138–139.
105. "Bank Officers and Director Liability — Regulatory Actions," 39 *The Business Lawyer* 1021 (1984).
106. "Statistics on the Federal Response to Criminal Misconduct by Bank Officers, Directors, and Insiders: A Staff Analysis," Subcommittee on Commerce, Consumer and Monetary Affairs, May 2, 1984.
107. *Gibbons v. Anderson*, 80 F. 345 (C.C. Mich., 1897).

Appendix A: The Board Meeting*

Attendance at board meetings is a basic obligation of directors. The board's regularly scheduled meetings should take top priority in a director's schedule to assure that the board benefits from the director's contribution and that the director is protected from certain liabilities stemming from negligence.

RESPONSIBILITIES

The board's role is to advise and counsel the CEO, listen critically to management's reports, review results, and offer suggestions for improvement. The directors have a responsibility to be adequately informed about all aspects of the bank's affairs and to come to the board meetings prepared to analyze, discuss, and review the bank's performance, as well as to propose changes to enhance the bank's growth. Unless the directors are adequately informed, they cannot satisfactorily fulfill their duties. In addition, the time that directors can devote to board meetings is limited, so the meeting will be more productive if they are knowledgeable about the issues.

The chairman of the board, with assistance from the CEO and other board members, usually takes responsibility for writing a good agenda for the meeting, for informing the directors of the

---

*This material is adapted from *The Director's Notebook*, ABA (1979).

agenda items, and for supplying all necessary information and documents to the other board members.

The CEO is responsible for executing the board's decisions. The CEO should bring issues dealing with strategy or resource allocation to the board at the beginning of the period when management is working on them, to give the board an opportunity to provide input, help structure the issue, and develop the issue as work progresses on it. Bringing issues to the board for preliminary debate makes maximum use of the board's expertise.

The chairman of the board is the key to the board's successful operation. The effective chairman must understand not only the substance of the issues to be discussed, but also the dynamics of the meeting process. The chairman must encourage all points of view, ensure that the issues are fully developed, and be sure the directors have access to all the facts, not just those facts that serve special management interests.

ANNUAL BOARD CALENDAR

An annual calendar should be made available to each director at the beginning of the year. The annual calendar is usually developed by the CEO in conjunction with the chairman of the board, and then presented to the board for discussion and approval.

The calendar schedules many essential items that require only annual or semiannual review. One of its chief uses is to ensure that the board accomplishes such routine tasks as approving charge-offs and monitoring lending activities, without devoting excessive time to these housekeeping tasks.

The calendar is unique to each bank, and it should include dates for board meetings, directors' committee meetings, periodic reviews of policy statements, shareholders' meetings, and special reports.

Reports on the following areas may be submitted annually, semiannually, or at irregular intervals to the board, either following a particular occurrence, when board approval is necessary, or when the matter should be brought in timely fashion to the board's attention:

- affirmative action/EEO
- annual budget
- audit program
- bank plan
- board candidates
- capital and dividend plan
- insurance and surety coverage
- management succession
- marketing plan
- pending legislation
- pending litigation
- personnel/compensation policy
- security/emergency preparedness policy
- tax plan

Several actions, such as changing the articles of association or changing the surplus account, can be taken only by the stockholders. These and related issues are attended to at the annual stockholders' meeting, in addition to the election or reelection of the members of the board. Under certain circumstances, special stockholders' meetings can be called. Any stockholder or group of stockholders representing more than a specified minimum of the bank's stock can call a special meeting to discuss any pertinent issue.

BOARD MEETING AGENDA

For a board meeting to be purposeful, there must be: 1) specific meeting dates, set well in advance; 2) clear role definitions and standards of performance for the chairman, the CEO, and the directors; 3) systematic, advance provision for all the supporting information the board needs to function properly; and 4) a well-defined agenda.

To prepare a well-defined agenda, the chairman of the board and/or the CEO should:

- limit the agenda items to important issues that demand board review and/or approval;

- single out any item of special interest to the group, perhaps in a cover note;

- add agenda items at the beginning of the meeting, if a significant concern of the directors is not scheduled to be addressed;

- give policy considerations more emphasis than operational details;

- give the directors an opportunity to offer input into future agendas;

- allot sufficient time for each major item to be thoroughly discussed;

- allow flexibility in the agenda, so it can be adapted to the needs of the meeting;

- schedule the order of agenda items, with these questions in mind:

  — Do some items demand immediate attention and early scheduling? Can others wait until the next meeting, if necessary?

  — Do some matters require resolution before others can be discussed? (For example, the delinquent and substandard loan report should be evaluated before the lending policy is reviewed.)

  — Does the agenda include a topic of interest and concern that will evoke a lot of discussion? (If so, it should be discussed after the other necessary work is finished.)

  — Do any issues unite or divide the board? (It is usually a good idea to end the meeting with a unifying theme.); and

- indicate the proper action to be taken on each item, that is, a decision, approval, or advice and discussion.

Exhibit 4
Sample Agenda for a Board of Directors' Meeting

December 6, 19—

Approve Minutes of Previous Meeting

Comparative Financial Statements

- Statement of Condition
- Statement of Income
- Schedule of Expense Operating Ratios

New Loans and Commitments

Delinquency Report and Substandard Loan Review

Loans Recommended for Charge-Off

Schedule of Investments

Auditor's Report

- Overdraft Report
- Cash Items
- Tellers' Over and Short Report

Committee Reports

Old Business

New Business

- Examination Report
- Correspondence
- Personnel Actions and Salaries
- Officers' and Directors' Borrowings
- Insider Transactions
- Interest Rates/Competitive Conditions
- Topical Issues
- Physical Purchases of a Capital Nature

Officer's presentation: Department—past, present, future

CONFIDENTIALITY

Comprehensive minutes are taken at each meeting by a board-appointed secretary. Included in the minutes or in a separate confidential document should be exhibits and documents used at the meeting and a record of each director's

Exhibit 5
Sample Agenda for a Board of Directors' Meeting

August 6, 19—

Minutes of Previous Meeting
    Briefly Review Highlights
    Approve

Financial Condition:
    Assess, through:
        Statement of Condition
        Income and Expense Statement
        Ratio Analysis

Asset/Liability Management Policy
    Evaluate policy
    Discuss/approve recommended changes

New Loans and Commitments
    Review minutes of Loan and Discount Committee Meeting
    Approve new loans

Delinquent Trend Report
    Briefly review delinquent and substandard loans
    Analyze valuation reserve for loans
    Approve recommendations for additional reserves

Break

Internal Audit Report
    Review findings
    Identify/approve course of action for significant discrepancies

Delinquency Trends
    Determine necessity of subsequent lending policy review

Charge-Off Recommendations
    Approve recommendations

Correspondent Banking Relationships
    Present brief oral report on adequacy of services rendered by
        First National

EFTS
    Discuss proposal for implementing an electronic funds transfer
        system within next 5 years

opinions and voting pattern for that meeting. Usually, a simple majority is needed to carry a vote on the board. However, bylaws, articles of incorporation, or state or federal regulation may require a minimum percentage vote on specific issues.

Sending directors pertinent material prior to the actual meeting can expedite the board's discussion and decision-making. Because of the confidential nature of some material, certain documents may have to be kept inside the bank. However, many supporting documents can be sent to the directors in advance. Selected readings from banking publications not readily accessible to outside directors and internal memos concerning policy issues are two examples of such supporting documents. Some banks also mail comparative financial statements to the board before the meeting. The purpose of this material is to provide general economic and banking background information and/or more specific information on policy issues that will be discussed at the meeting.

Business discussed at a board meeting is confidential. In some banks, directors are not allowed to take documents received at board meetings out of the bank. The pertinent documents are supplied in loose-leaf binders at the beginning of the meeting and collected at the end. Other banks take the position that the directors would not violate the confidential nature of the business discussed and do not impose this restriction.

Appendix B: Policy Formulation and Evaluation Checklists*

This section, which is designed to assist the board with policy formulation and the evaluation of management performance, contains checklists that cover the following areas of bank policy:

- comparative financial statements
- lending
- investments
- delinquent and substandard loans
- charge-off recommendations
- auditing
- marketing

The "Policy Considerations" section of each checklist highlights the factors that are essential in maintaining an effective policy statement. The "Evaluation" section of each checklist identifies specific points for assessing the bank's current position. For example, in the checklist on lending, the policy considerations section lists items that are crucial for the smooth, profitable operation of the bank. The evaluation section lists specific points that should be evaluated periodically, such as

---

*This material is adapted from *The Director's Notebook*, ABA (1979).

the investment portfolio's marketability, volume mix, and liquidity.

Although reviewing monthly financial statements and reports on lending, investments, auditing, and so forth are processes with which directors are most familiar, the more crucial function of these review processes is to gain an in-depth, overall view of the bank's performance—a view that will provide the basis for evaluating and adopting more effective policy statements and long-range plans.

Checklist 1
Comparative Financial Statements

Policy Considerations

☑ Coordination of policies impacting current financial position; asset/liability, lending, investments, bank plan

☑ Capital position

☑ Liquidity position

☑ Comparison of current position to past performance
   —self-comparison
   —industry levels

☑ Community development responsibilities

Evaluation—Financial Condition

(i.e., Statement of Condition and Detailed Income and Expense Statement)

☑ Capital adequacy

☑ Liquidity (ability to meet normal deposit outflows and loan demands)
   —cash position
   —short-term investment funds
   —risk assets

☑ Examination of:
   —asset mix
     • cash
     • investments
     • loans
   —deposit mix
     • demand
     • savings
     • time

☑ Moderate use of federal and/or other rate-sensitive borrowed funds

☑ Adequate loan loss provision

☑ Operating ratios to assess bank's financial condition and performance
   —loan/deposit ratio
   —demand/time ratio
   —return on assets
   —return on equity
   —other

☑ Comparison of actual performance to budget projections

Checklist 2
Lending

Policy Considerations

☑ Competitive market conditions (i.e., clear identification of primary and secondary trade areas)

☑ Determination of acceptable level of risk (e.g., rating of risk)

☑ Desirable/feasible rate of return on lending activity

☑ Loan spread

☑ Legal/regulatory requirements

☑ Balanced risk among portfolios

☑ Contributions to community development

☑ Participation of directors in new business development

Evaluation—New Loans and Commitments

☑ Money market conditions/economic forecast

☑ Sound credit standards

☑ Lending policy adhered to or limited number of exceptions

☑ Loan mix reviewed by category

☑ Pricing (yields vs. cost of funds)

☑ Report of loans made since last meeting, including:
  —total indebtedness
  —interest rate
  —nature of security/collateral/guaranty
  —other pertinent information

☑ Review of new business development/lending

Checklist 3
Investments

Policy Considerations

☑ Type and quality of investments
—appropriate yields
—liquidity requirements
—pledging requirements
—tax considerations
—market analyst's ratings

☑ Legal/regulatory restrictions

☑ Maturity mix (scheduling appropriate maturities and establishing maximum maturity limit)

☑ Balance risk within portfolio
—diversification/concentration standards

☑ Consideration of community/state investment offerings

Evaluation—Investment Portfolio

☑ Investment policy adhered to, or limited number of exceptions

☑ Appropriate earning asset mix (e.g., investments/loans)

☑ Portfolio criteria
—volume mix
—liquidity constraints
—yield

☑ Current tax position
—tax-exempt securities (e.g., appropriate volume, quality, yield, and maturity)

☑ Investment strategy
—money market conditions
—economic forecast

☑ Portfolio valuation (book value vs. market value)

☑ Portfolio marketability

Checklist 4
Delinquent and Substandard Loans

Policy Considerations

☑ Loan "watch list" with periodic review
   —substandard
   —classified
   —nonaccruing

☑ Delinquency trend report

☑ Appraisal of collection effort
   —percentage of charge-offs
   —industry level comparison (e.g., consumer loans)

Evaluation—Reports, Trends

☑ Review of the following:
   —loan history
     • name of borrower
     • outstanding principal
     • amount past due
     • due date
     • servicing officer
   —collectibility
     • amount of potential loss
     • reasons for delinquency
     • actions taken to ensure collection

☑ Directors encouraged to offer insight that may aid collection

☑ Delinquency trends
   —reason(s) for overall change
   —evaluation of lending officer(s)
   —review of lending policy, as required

☑ Review of level of reserve for loan losses (e.g., ratio of loan loss reserve to outstanding loan ratio)

Checklist 5
Charge-Off Recommendations

Policy Considerations

☑ Clear guidelines for determining charge-off recommendations
    —service officers' written recommendations
    —subsequent approval by regulatory authorities
    —tax considerations

☑ Provision for permanent recordkeeping to
    —monitor Regulation B compliance
    —continue collection efforts

Evaluation—Reports, Trends

☑ Periodic review of loan charge-offs

☑ Review of "overdrafts" and "bad checks" recommended for charge-off

☑ Review of adequacy of bad-debt reserve after charge-offs

☑ Report of recovery efforts detailed on a periodic basis

☑ Comparison of charge-off level to industry trends

☑ Review of lending and charge-off policy, as required

Checklist 6
Auditing

Policy Considerations

☑ Audit program to cover internal controls concerning financial and operational procedures, to
—provide reasonable assurance that book assets are safeguarded
—detect errors and irregularities and promptly correct them
—ensure bank security
—protect nonbook assets
  • charged-off loans
  • depreciated assets
—comply with management policies, laws, regulations, and sound fiduciary principles
—promote operational efficiency
—verify custodial items (e.g., dormant and escrow accounts, traveler's checks)

☑ Selection of audit program, to
—determine specifications of audit process
—coordinate internal and external audit processes

☑ Regulatory compliance

☑ Role of directors in audit process

Evaluation—Auditing Report

☑ Periodic review of audit process and findings
—course of action identified to deal with any discrepancies, unusual findings, and recommended changes

☑ Review of audit program
—timing and scope vary unpredictably

☑ Direct verification of loans and deposits

☑ Adherence to basic principles of auditing and control

☑ Maintenance of independent auditor

☑ Presentation of follow-up report to board

Checklist 7
Marketing

Policy Considerations

☑ Responsibilities to community
    —role of service in community's growth
    —marketing efforts a reflection of community's economic
    conditions

☑ Legal/regulatory requirements

☑ Marketing plan
    —competitive environment
    —growth potential
    —effects on other bank policies

☑ Marketing education (e.g., directors, officers, employees)
    —technological advances
    —knowledge of services
    —cross-selling

Evaluation—Marketing Plan

☑ Consumer perceptions of bank/community image
    —research
    —informal feedback from community
    —customer complaints

☑ Evaluation of marketing plan objectives/results

☑ Appraisal of market share (e.g., deposits, loans)

Index

A

C

Fines, 101, 124
FIRA, see Financial Institutions
  Regulatory and Interest Rate
  Control Act
Float, 33
Focus on the Bank Director
  (ABA)
  first edition of, v
  present edition of, v-vi
Forgery, 99, 105-106
Fraud, 85, 106, 117-119, 122
  management, 44
Freedom, 78
  of choice, 11
  of expression, 59
Free enterprise system, 5
Fringe benefits, 83
Functional regulation, 51-52
Funds, 44
  bank, 122-123
  borrowed, 32, 36, 38, 46-47
  for business expansion, 6
  cost of, 18
  mismanagement of, 79
  protection of, 48, 68
  sources of, 30
  transfer of, 11, 17-18, 23
  useable, 23
Funds held in trust, lending of,
  125
Furniture, 31, 39
Futures brokerage, 19

G

Garn St Germain Depository
  Institutions Act of 1982, 11, 50
Garrison, Gene, vii
Geographic areas for doing
  business, 5, 7, 9, 25-26, 43,
  50-51, 75
Gifts, 123, 125
Glass-Steagall Act of 1933, 78
Goals, 54
Good faith, 65, 97, 100-101
Goods, durable, 16
Government agencies, 6, 8

Government customers, 6
Graft, 123
Gratuities, 101
Growth, 29

H

Health plans, 83
Hearings, public, 129
Hiring, 25, 72, 80
Holding companies
  bank, see Bank holding
  companies
  multibank, 8-9
Holidays, 83
Home financing, 10
Homestead associations, 113
Housing, 7
Human resources, 25

I

Ignorance of the law, 105
Imprisonment, 101, 123-124
Income, 33-34, 40-41, 54
  audits of, 85
  fee, 13, 29, 37-38, 54
  interest, 38
  non-interest, 39
  operating, 37
  retirement, 7
Income statements, 30, 37-41
Income taxes, 32, 40
Indemnification, director, 66, 96,
  133-134, 136
Individual accounts, 3
Individual loans, 22, 31, 38
Individual pensions, 11
Individual Retirement Accounts
  (IRAs), 14-15, 83
Individuals, loans to, 15
Industrial banks, 113
Industrial development bonds, 51
Industrial loans, 31, 38
Inflation, 1, 7, 18, 29
Information, 72, 87
Inside directors, 59

Insider transactions, 101, 110-111,
    113-114, 117
Installment loans, 22
    commercial, 10
    retail, 10
Insurance, 40, 44, 63, 145
    director, 66, 96, 133-134, 136
    liability, 134
Insurance brokerage, 19, 51
Insurance underwriting, 19, 51
Insured status, termination of, 128
Integrity, 138
Intent in violations, 104-106
Interest
    accrued, 36
    on demand deposits, 109
    on deposits, 14
    deregulation of ceilings on, 18
    on loans, 34
    on securities, 38
Interest bearing liabilities, 32
Internal control, 79
Interest earnings, 6
Interest expenses, 38-39
Interest income, 38
Interest margin, 39
Interest rates
    fluctuating, 26
    increases in, 46
    minimum, 75
    volatile, 1, 18
Interlocking directorates, 112-113
Internal controls, 79, 85-86
Internal friction, 79
International banking, specialists
    in, 6
International banking services, 9
Investment decision-making,
    23-24
Investment philosophy, 78-79
Investment policies, 74, 76-78
Investment portfolios, 23, 34,
    76-77, 137
Investments, 3, 17, 23, 27, 30-31,
    155
    real estate, 51
    short-term, 33
    specialists in, 6

Investment securities, 34
IRAs, *see* Individual Retirement
    Accounts

K

Keogh accounts, 14-15
Knowledge in violations, 104-106,
    136, 138

L

Labor relations, 83-84
Land, 31
Law
    antitrust, 66, 95, 119-120
    case, *see* Common law
    common, *see* Common law
    criminal, *see* Criminal law
    federal, *see* Federal law
    ignorance of the, 105
    securities, 66, 95, 117-119
    statutory, *see* Statutory law
Laws, vi, 35
    enforcement of, 54, 135
    state, *see* State laws
    wage and hour, 81-82
Lawsuits, 133
Leasehold improvements, 31, 39
Leases, 22, 26, 31, 39-40
Legal responsibilities of bank
    directors, vi, 54, 57, 59, 62,
    65-66, 70, 95-138
Legislation, 145
Lending, 3, 154
    of funds held in trust, 125
    truth in, 17
Lending limits, 74-75
Lending policies, 74-76
Letter agreements, 128
Liabilities, 30, 32, 35-36
    audits of, 85
    interest bearing, 32
    non-interest bearing, 32
Liability
    civil, *see* Civil liability
    collection, v-vi

Minorities, 62, 70, 80-81
Misapplication of bank funds,
122-123, *see also* Defalcations
Misrepresentations, 117, 119
Mobility, 82
Monetary Control Act, *see*
Depository Institutions
Deregulation and Monetary
Control Act of 1980
Monetary policy, 49
Money, 3-4
Money market, 76
Money market accounts, 14-15,
32, 38
Money market certificates, 14-15
Money market funds, 10-11, 50
Money orders, 17
Money penalties, 129
Money rate checking, 32
Money supply, 4, 46
Monopoly, 119
Mortgage companies, 10-11
Mortgage loans, 74-75
Mortgages, 22
commercial, 11
real estate, 10
residential, 6, 10-11, 70
Multibank holding companies,
8-9
Multiple expansion of bank
deposits, 4-5
Municipal debt issues, 6, 28, 31,
38, 76
Mutual funds, 11, 19, 51-52
Mutual savings banks, 10
federal, 49

N

National Bank Act (12 U.S.C. 84),
101, 105-108, 124
Section 53 of, 104
*National Bank of Boston et al. v.
Bellotti* (1978), 124
National banks, vi, 8, 44-45, 48,
59, 61, 65, 115, 123
Negligence, 121, 137

Negotiable order of withdrawal
(NOW) accounts, 14, 32, 38-39,
49, 109
super, 14, 50
Net worth, audits of, 85
Nonbank institutions, 1, 51
Nondepository institutions, 9-12
Notes, 80
capital, 32, 36, 38
Treasury, 6
NOW accounts, *see* Negotiable
order of withdrawal accounts

O

OCC, *see* Office of the
Comptroller of the Currency
Occurancy expenses, 39, 68
Office of the Comptroller of the
Currency (OCC), 8, 12, 44-45,
47, 92, 95, 127, 133-134, 136,
138
Regulation 9, 78
Office supplies, 37
Operating efficiency, 90
Operating procedures, 5, 68
Operating ratios, 91-92
Operations, 24, 27
Ordinary care, 97-100
Ordinary diligence, 97-100
Organization, 1, 21-28
Organizational methods, 25-28
Outside directors, 59
Overdrafts, 85, 112, 122

P

Parent corporations, 7
Payments, making and collecting
of, 3-4, 13, 16-17
Payrolls, corporate, 3
Payroll, services, 25
Penalties
civil, 128
of criminal law, 121-122
money, 129
Pension plans, 83

Pension Reform Act of 1974, 78
Pensions
  corporate, 11, 23
  individual, 11
Performance, 21-22, 41, 71, 86-92
Performance analysis services, 24
Personal liability, v-vi, 21, 70, 76, 85-138
Personal loans, 31, 38
Personal property taxes, 39
Personnel, 6, 22, 25
Personnel policies, 74, 79-84, 145
Peters, Reed A., vi
Phone, banking by, 16
Photo detection, 84
Plans, long-range, 54, 72, 145
Point-of-sale terminals, 16
Policies, 21-22, 71-85
  appraisal, 75
  emergency preparedness, 145
  investment, 74, 76-78
  lending, 74-76
  security, 74, 84, 145
  staff, 25
  trust, 74, 78-79
Policy evaluation, 151-159
Policy formulation, 151-159
Political activities, 124-125
Portfolios
  investment, 23, 34, 76-77, 137
  loan, 34, 137
  real estate, 35
Premises, 31, 35, 109
Premiums, promotional, 115
Prestige, 62
Pricing, 24, 43, 50, 154
Printing, 37, 40
Prison terms, 101, 123-124
Privacy, 69, 114
Procedures, 50
Product development, 24
Productivity, 51, 79
Products, 1, 3-4, 7, 12-19, 26, 29, 43, 50-53
  expansion of, 18-19
Product specialists, 26
Professional experience, 60

Profitability, 1, 18-19, 22, 29-41, 44, 52, 72, 76-77
  measures of, 41
Profitability ratios, 41
Profits, 29, 37, 105
  net, 108
  undivided, 32
Promotion, 24, 80
Promotional premiums, 115
Property values, 107
Prudent person rule, 79, 97-100, 136
Public disclosure, 101
Public hearings, 129
Public relations, 24
  specialists in, 6
Public responsibility, 67, 69-70
Purloining of bank funds, 123

Q

Qualifying shares, 61
Quality of investment securities, 34

R

Raw materials, 3-4, 15
Real estate, bank, 109
Real estate brokerage, 19, 51
Real estate development, 51
Real estate equity, 19
Real estate investments, 51
Real estate loans, 3, 15-16, 26-27, 31, 38, 74-75, 107
Real estate mortgages, 10
Real estate portfolios, 35
Real Estate Settlement Procedures Act, 76
Reasonable persons, 97
Receivers, 47
Records, 87
Recruitment, 25
Reform, regulatory, 50-53
Regulation, functional, 51-52
Regulation 9 (OCC), 78